COMMUNICATION AND INTIMACY IN MARRIAGE

EXERCISES TO RESOLVE CONFLICT WITH YOUR SPOUSE, GROW TOGETHER, STRENGTHEN YOUR MARRIAGE, AND IMPROVE YOUR RELATIONSHIP

PAUL H. MENDOZA

CONTENTS

Introduction 1
Chapter 1 3
    Communication In Budding Relationships 3
Chapter 2 9
    How To Repair Broken Trust 9
Chapter 3 16
    The Six Most Common Mistakes In Communication To Avoid 16
Chapter 4 25
    The Why And How Of Empathy 25
Chapter 5 34
    The Importance Of Work On Yourself First 34
Chapter 6 40
    Communication At The Beginning Of Budding Relationships 40
Chapter 7 50
    Approaching A Group For Rapport Building 50
Chapter 8 59
    The Importance Of Empathy 59
Chapter 9 66
    Improve Your Communication Using Emotional Management 66
Conclusion 75

INTRODUCTION

If you're wondering whether ego is playing a part in preventing effective communication from taking place with your partner, take a look at the following signs:

- You're constantly blaming your partner for everything, without taking any responsibility for your actions. It is always someone else's fault.
- You find yourself playing the "victim card" far too often in your relationship.
- You get jealous easily, which leads to a lot of arguments and blame. Jealousy tends to cause a lot of drama within your relationships and causing a lot of toxic energy to manifest itself.
- You fear being rejected by your partner, especially when they seem to be achieving more than you do.
- You feel the need to have the last word all the time, in every argument especially. It is always about you and your opinions, and you don't spend enough time thinking about how your partner feels or what they have to say.

Kicking Ego Out the Front Door Once and for All

If you're reading this book, then you know communication skills is something that you need to work on to improve your relationships. If ego has been a force that you've been dealing with until this point, then there's only one thing left for you to do - kick it out the front door where it belongs.

Ego does not belong in your relationship. It never has, and it never will. To get rid of ego once and for all and start improving communication between you and your significant other, the following strategies are something you need to start working on right now:

- *There's No Need to Always Be Right* - Sure, being right feels good, but you don't *always* have to be right all the time. It is okay to be wrong every now and again. Yes, it may be hard for you to do in the beginning, but this is something you *must* do if you want to start seeing any kind of improvement in your relationship. No one is perfect, and you shouldn't expect yourself to be perfect. There will be times when you find yourself in the wrong. Instead of becoming defensive, use these situations to learn from what went wrong.

- *You Don't Need to Be Superior* - Do you have this need to always be the one who's in charge? The one who's in control? Do you want to be better than everyone? That's ego at work there again. Instead of trying to compete to be better than everyone else all the time, especially your partner, why not focus on yourself and what *you can do to become a better person* overall? That would be the healthier approach not just for your relationships, but for your everyday life too.

- *Give Up Being Easily Offended* - If you find yourself getting offended far too easily, even over the simplest things, that's ego working behind the scenes again. People are not out to offend you on purpose, especially your partner, so it's time to start practicing a little bit more tolerance. Make it a conscious practice, and remind yourself that everyone expresses themselves differently. When you practice tolerance, it makes it easier to have effective conversations with your partner that don't escalate into arguments.

- *Be Forgiving* - Gandhi once said that *"forgiveness is something that is attributed to the strong"*. He was right. Forgiveness is one of the most powerful tools you could possess to make letting go of your ego easier. Not only will you eventually gain the ability to forgive others over time when you let go of your ego, but you'll also learn to forgive yourself. You'll learn acceptance, and you'll learn how to be much happier when you let go of all the anger that resides within you.

CHAPTER 1

Communication in Budding Relationships

Who doesn't enjoy the feeling of being in a budding relationship? The fresh flush of love, being wooed and swept off the feet by your potential make! The feel good endorphin rush in the brain that keeps you happy, driven and positive all the time! For many people, this is the most perfect phase of a relationship, which only goes downhill from here. Well, not really. The relationship can solidify and get even stronger if you communicate effectively during the initial stages.

Here are some of the best communication tips for a budding romantic relationship

1. Own Past Mistakes

Work your way through past mistakes and disappointments rather than pretending they didn't exist. If something went wrong in the past relationship owing to your mistake, accept it to avoid repeating it in the current relationship or you're going down heartbreak alley all over again.

For example, if you pretended to be something you were not in a bid to put your best foot forward and impress your date, which was later discovered and the relationship ended on a sour note, be genuine this time. Reveal your real, genuine, honest self to the other person in an attempt to undo or mend past relationship mistakes. Own it or accept responsibility for past mistakes and move ahead. If you have the option of seeing a therapist or attending an assistance program, consider opting for it to overcome past issues and start the new relationship on a fresh slate. Clear the cob webs, clear your feelings and begin on a more positive note.

2. Acquire Skills Gradually

The truth is you will learn certain communication patterns only over a period of time by communicating more and more with the person. This means you'll need to invest time in listening to your partner, understanding them, knowing what they like or dislike, their views about major things in life.

Make it your main objective to understand them. Take time out to actively listen to them. Put your ego and need to be right all the time aside. Your primary intention should be to understand the person and be understood. Rather than constructing your own clever responses, focus on what your partner is trying to convey.

3. Avoid Bringing the Past Into The Present

We are often tempted to bring out past into the present through a series of assumptions and comparisons. Sometimes, unknowingly, you may carry the anger, frustration or hurt of a previous relationship into a new relationship, which is grossly unfair to the new partner. You may not have done the groundwork to overcome the pitfall of the former relationship, the price of which may be your current relationship.

Avoid making assumptions based on past relationships by not listening carefully to your partner. He/she may be trying to communicate something totally different than what you assume using your past relationship filters. Give them time, space and confidence to speak by listening to them and more importantly, understanding them correctly.

Constantly interrupting them or dishing off their feelings/emotions as unfounded or invalid can prove disastrous. Don't make sweeping statements such as "you never …. "or "you always." Keep it thoughtful and unfiltered. For a while just listen to them without trying to judge them. The trouble in budding relationships is we quickly try to compare and judge potential partners rather than attempting to understand them. Observe them with more understanding tinted glasses, and communication will flow.

4. Avoid Oversharing

I know people who in a bid to prove to their partner that they are really serious about the relationship end up sharing much more than they should. They think it makes them come across as human, vulnerable and endearing. Of course, honesty and openness are appreciated in any relationship. However, there is a right time for sharing everything. You don't have to plunge into the relationship head on and reveal your deepest, darkest and unknown secrets to your new partner.

Since they are also getting to know you and may not understand the secrets in their right context, you run the risk of creeping them out and ending the relationship. Give them time to know and understand you to view your secrets in the right context. In a situation where they don't have any previous information to go by, there is a high chance that they may not understand what you are trying to communicate.

When we meet people for the first time or for a couple of times, the information we get is generally overemphasized because we don't know any better. There is no foundation or basis against which we can view what a new partner just communicated. When you share personal and deep secrets, the other person will give these details more significance than needed.

On the other hand, when you spend more time with a person in the long haul, you have a larger context to view what they've just stated. Their quirks, actions, thoughts and behaviors can be viewed in the correct light.

Of course, you want to share more intimate or vulnerable details about yourself to reveal your trust in the other person. So what's the middle way? Allow yourself to be occasionally vulnerable when the mood is perfect or you find your partner sharing vulnerable details too.

However, don't make it too revealing a conversation prematurely. If at all you end up sharing more than required, admit that you are feeling slightly insecure about whatever you've told them. Their reaction will help you determine if they display understanding towards what you've shared. This can be your clue to sharing or not sharing more in the future (if there is a future after what you've shared that is lol).

5. Don't Come On Too Strong For Heaven's Sake

Don't come across as too available or eager to jump into the relationship through your verbal and non-verbal communication. The partner will wonder whether you want to be in a relationship with them or you are simply desperate to be in a relationship, even with a wall. It doesn't really tell the other person that you love or adore them.

Though it may seem overhyped, there is some element of truth in the notion that we crave something we can't easily have even more. If you appear desperate and go all out to please your partner by making yourself too available or too in their face all the time, you may not be doing it right. We strive harder for rewards that appear beyond our reach. Coming on too strongly can be a terrible turn-off for your partner. It will make them lose interest, and they'll communicate with you in a more disinterested manner. People will fast lose interest if you come across as too overbearing.

Also, you'd like to spend more time together with your partner to understand them without coming across as too eager. Talk to them and set expectations right in the beginning to ensure you both are aligned in the same direction. Determine how often you want to meet or how much time you wish to spend together. Once expectations are clarified, there is little room for disappointment, miscommunication and frustration.

6. Pray Don't Be Dismissive

This is another extreme of the above point. Sometimes, in their need to come across as more desirable or irresistible, people purposefully limit or restrict communication with their budding partners. It is the subtle art of showing people we really don't care. Don't be available all the time but don't cut off someone to establish your importance or superiority. Some people assume that they'll know instantly whether there's a connection with the other person. Guess what? It may not always be true. At times, you just need to give it more time to understand that the other person is perfect for you. There may not be a Eureka or ringing bells, falling flowers moment. You may need weeks to determine if the relationship will work.

Don't dismiss a potential partner or budding relationship simply because you didn't feel it right in the beginning or even after a few days. Understand that relationships need time to nurture, which can be done through communication and understanding. Just because it doesn't feel right or perfect in the beginning doesn't mean it isn't meant to be. The best of relationships can grow and thrive over a period of time if nurtured with love, communication and understanding.

It happens on television shows and movies but real life is different! I know several mediocre or even downright disastrous first dates that transformed into awesome relationships only because the people involved gave it another chance. Give the person more time before dismissing him or her.

7. Revealing Insecurity

If you ask me to mention my number one relationship killer in the early days, it is revealing your insecurity. When you start dating someone, there is plenty of grey area, along with uncertainties and assumptions. If you have any genuine concerns, talk it out with your partner. However, it isn't fair to make your new partner the target of your insecurities, when they don't deserve it. Try to get to the bottom of your feelings.

Where have your feelings originated from? Why do you feel the way you feel? Was an earlier relationship or person responsible for making you feel the way you do? Did an incident or occurrence in a previous relationship ruin things for you? Has your previous partner been unfaithful to you? Don't allow jealousy or insecurity to determine how you treat the other person. Instead, address the root cause of the issue. You can deal with it on your own and enlist your partner's help too.

Speak to them in a frank, open and candid manner about how you feel. Tell them you don't want to come across as insecure or jealous but a few incidents or past relationships have turned you into a more insecure person, and that you are genuinely working on it. You can also tell them how you need their help in the process.

Sometimes, it is great to witness some mistakes early in the relationship because they offer some realistic or practical tests for couples. Do you communicate effectively as a couple? Are you as a couple apologetic or accusatory? These are all indicators which will help you lay the foundation of a healthy relationship.

Don't fret if you just started seeing someone and hit a slight roadblock. Work through your couple mistakes. Even if you make a mistake, view it as an opportunity to grow together instead of giving up even without trying and throwing away a relationship which could have been wonderful in the long run.

8. Don't Get Defensive

When we open up to a new relationship, the temptation to jump to our own defensive is pretty high. If a new mate challenges something you say or do, you want to prove to them that you are right so they don't view you in a negative light. However, being defensive doesn't always help. On the contrary, you'll come across as egoistic, dogmatic and self-centered. Position yourself as someone who is open to hearing different perspectives and points of view.

Demonstrate your ability to listen, appreciate and understand your new partner's perspective even if you don't necessarily believe in it. Be open to discussions and listen calmly to the other person's perspective. Own up to your thoughts or actions rather than defending them and making a fool of yourself. If the person doesn't accept you, trust me, you are much better off without them.

Learn the subtle art of communicating without getting defensive. This is even truer in a relatively budding relationship. Build a foundation for a mutually respectful and loving relationship. Even if you don't agree about some things, don't attack or misjudge the other person.

realize that you have gotten rid of past baggage and are coming back into the relationship totally fresh.

- **Be honest**

If your partner is interested in patching up their marriage, then at this point they'll be asking questions, digging into your sins, wanting to know precisely what happened, even though you have explained before many times over. But you must be honest. It would really look bad on you to run away with a lie and be caught in a dead end. As long as you are telling the truth, the story will fall into place. At this point you should also give perspective to your actions. Let your spouse understand what motivated you, influenced you, who else had been around. Pass yourself off as a weak human being who got carried away and indulged in something you shouldn't have but also add that you are ready to pay the price of betraying your partner.

- **Try to charm them**

Since they are your spouse, you must know the right buttons to push and have them giggling. Make them taste of your charisma once more. This is what they risk losing should they reject your apology. Try as much as you can to get into their well of emotions and convince them for a second chance. If you are too charming, you might see your partner fighting off a smile, which is a really good sign.

- **Open the floor for them**

Should your partner decide to trust you again, sorry, decide to give you a chance to see whether they can trust you again, they will first have to give you a lecture. Maybe warn you that it's your last chance and after that you will lose them. Be attentive and agree to their every command. If they are crazy, like the right type of crazy, they might order you to lie down on your stomach so that they whip some sense into you. Do it.

Tips on keeping love alive

Love is the glue that holds marriages together. When you run out of love, your marriage either crumbles or you become a miserable person; both nasty options. Thus, it is important to learn about ways of keeping your love alive for the long term.

- **Don't stop dating**

When you first met each other, you used to hit the restaurants to do dinner and cocktails. But when you got married, the dates stopped, and home life took over. Know what? You shouldn't have stopped dating. Yes, you are married now, but you can keep going out on couple's dates. You don't necessarily have to go to fancy restaurants. You may renovate your compound and create a section where you can have dates that last even an entire day. If you love someone you will always share a connection with them. But that's not enough, for in order to be deeply connected, you will have to use a sprinkling of imagination. Thus, ensure that you are applying your imagination in your marriage so as to keep the love alive.

- **Don't stop going on honeymoons**

We are about breaking the rules. Who says that newlyweds have monopoly of honeymoons? Even couples who have been together for ages should go for honeymoons when they want to. Every year ensure that you and your significant other travel away for honeymoon. Leave the kids behind. Such experiences will help you understand one another be the best couple. Honeymoons are expensive if you are traveling overseas and staying in five star hotels. But you don't need to cross continents for your honeymoon. If you lack the financial muscle of traveling overseas, just look for a domestic spot, and go there by train or car.

- **Unplug from social media**

Social media is responsible for the demise of many marriages. Thanks to websites like Facebook and Twitter, people now are competing with a global audience, as each one of them struggles to show their awesomeness, their perfect sweet heart, their wonderful marriage, and so on. Thus, when people log on Facebook and see all these pictures, it tugs at their self-esteem. Social media is awash with busybodies who have nothing to do with their lives, thus they result to creating drama. In order to avoid racing against others, you might want to uninstall all these social media apps, and be real with your partner.

- **Take a bath together**

Simple things like taking a bath together can have a profound effect on a couple. The beauty of it is that it is free. And you can embark on this activity on a daily basis. Since you are lovers, don't be afraid of stretching your imagination. Take turns washing each other. When you scrub her back, she pays back with scrubbing your legs, and washing your back. Make it as fun as can be. Every day after work you may arrange for a sea salt bath and then proceed into your candle-lit bedroom for a magical night. Creating such authentic experiences draws a couple closer to one another.

- **Feed one another**

When you go out on dates in fancy restaurants you want to be the couple that stands out, but for good reason: feeding your spouse like a little baby. Sit across from each other in relatively small tables. And have the "baby" of the day fold their hands across their chest as the "momma" feeds her with her folk, or in extreme cases, leans across the table and actually administers food from their mouth, as if feeding a toothless baby.

- **Get lost in your spouse's eyes**

Develop a habit of staring deep into your spouse's eyes, so deep you can see their soul. But before you do that you want to first ensure that the environment is just right. Create a nice and cool ambience. Have your partner recline in a seat opposite yours. And then you can lean back and stare into their eyes. Ensure there's some light, background music to enhance the mood.

- ***Dance***

Who says that you have to have great dancing skills before you dance? After dinner, go round the table, pick your partner's hand and draw them to the dance floor. Dance your sorrows away. You may even get into the habit of randomly grabbing your spouse and engaging them in a dance. Simple things like dancing bring a couple closer to one another.

- **Massage each other**

When you have each other, you have no reason to seek costly massage services ever again. You only have to straddle your partner's back and work your fingers across their body, using generous amounts of massage oil. They will uuuh and ahhh as you grace your hands from one part to the other. Massages also help a couple understand what each other's body is like. Not to say that you will come across a part that seems nonhuman. But exploring your partner's body for a long time gives you a peek into their quirky traits, for instance, their weird erogenous zones.

- **Read love poems**

Most famous people who were into love were also big on poetry. William Shakespeare, Winston Churchill, William Faulkner… These were all accomplished men that loved women and also loved reading poems. Of course, not every person loves poetry. But you wouldn't know whether you love or hate it unless you tried. So, get in the habit of reading each other poems. It is a great method for killing time and also getting yourselves into the perfect mood for animated sex.

- **Write each other love letters**

A love letter is something to be cherished. They convey emotions in their rawest form. So, why don't you get into the habit of writing one another love letters and hide them in favorable places? Does it make it sense living in the same house and yet writing each other love letters? Yes, it does! If you find the use of paper and ink a little bothersome, you can always use your smartphone to send nice messages to your partner. What really matters is nurturing love and becoming fans of each other.

- **Play around**

Engage your partner in several games and act as though you were little kids. Don't let the years stop you from being a child at heart. If you have forgotten most your childhood games, research on the internet and you'll find more than enough games. Playing around not only brings you close to one another but also has a host of health benefits.

- **Be affectionate**

Never shout at your partner when communicating. Always ensure that you are near them, and speak in a most seductive manner. Play up your affectionate nature and make your partner feel as though they have a great effect on you, which is a real turn on. Also, when you are out in public, hold onto your spouse's arm, or snake your hand around their waist as you walk along.

- **Thank your partner**

When your partner does something thoughtful, you owe them a "Thank you!" Accepting favors from your partner and failing to say "Thank you" is uncouth behavior.

- **Forgive your partner**

Ruthless people with stone-like hearts either end up lonely or in some lock-up. But since you are not a ruthless person, you want to give your spouse another chance when they flop. Just as important is to keep them in check.

- **Send flowers**

Cliché, yes, but flowers never run out of style. Ensure that you are sending flowers to your significant other's place of work on the regular. Tuck naughty messages into the flowers so that your partner comes back home in the evening wanting a "fight."

- **Prepare their favorite meal**

Food is a big deal. If you are taking care of his stomach, he's likely to grow fond of you. Fix him his favorite meal every now and again and he'll be eternally grateful.

- **Be wild in bed**

Don't hesitate to try out new styles or do things that your lewd imagination suggests. Sex is one of the areas that need constant evolution. When you stick to a certain routine then your spouse will know all the tricks in your pockets and they will hate you for what you've become. So, keep your eyes on new trends to surprise your man with.

CHAPTER 3

The Six Most Common Mistakes in Communication to Avoid

When it comes to communication, we often get it wrong more times than right. Worse than that is how clueless we can be about why we were misunderstood or not listened to. Communication, as we have learned at this point, is a vital part of romantic relationships. As such, we must become mindful of the mistakes we inadvertently make in communication and take responsibility for those that are deliberate. Below are the six most common mistakes.

You Don't Listen to Your Partner When They Speak

Sometimes, it isn't about providing a solution to whatever issues they might have. Merely listening when they tell you what weighs heavily on their mind tells them that you care. It is also a sign of respect that you have for your partner and the relationship you both have committed to. Truly listening is not about sitting and pretending to be attentive. There are quite a few things that you must keep in mind to do.

Be Empathetic

When anyone speaks about emotional intelligence — the single factor that many successful leaders are credited with — they will always talk about empathy. But, what exactly is empathy and why is this important?

Simply put, it is the ability to stand where the other person is and feel exactly what they are trying to express in words. This is in contrast to sympathy, which is being able to feel sorry for what the person is going through. Going by this definition, it is clear which is the most effective at getting people to believe that you are truly listening. No one is born gifted with empathy, we all have a responsibility to develop it. It is a conscious effort to relate with your partner's feelings, even when you did not physically experience what you are being told.

When you are empathetic, you may convey this with a hug or by saying things in line with what your partner is talking about that show you are not detached.

Don't Interrupt

When it comes to that seemingly justifiable and near irresistible urge to point something out when your partner is talking to you, you should ignore it. It can feel right and appropriate, but it might come off to your partner as you not really being interested in what they have to say. Regardless of how incoherent or irrational what you're being told might seem, you ought to let them get it off their chest without cutting them off.

When you are talking to your partner, you must keep in mind that you are not in a debate. Tame your impatience. Many times, what people may have to say, if we only let them finish, tend to change the course and tone of the entire conversation. Holding your tongue for a few minutes more could let you look in hindsight and be thankful you did not jeer at your partner, have an outburst, or cut them off.

Be Careful with Unsolicited Advice

While it is not necessarily wrong to give advice to your partner when you think they need it, you should be careful to only do so when it is asked. Sometimes, all your partner needs from you is a listening ear. You should be able to do just that without dishing out from your well of wisdom and experience.

If you feel that you must give them advice, then be courteous in your approach to it. You absolutely do not want to appear like a know-it-all to your partner. Ask if it is alright that you give them advice concerning that particular issue and see if it is welcomed.

Appreciate Different Communication Styles

As simple as the topic of communication might seem to you, it is a lot more complex than that. Have you ever heard two people who, although are making the same points essentially, cannot seem to agree? They might argue for hours without knowing that they are on the same side. This is why listening is so important. It helps you to know your partner better and understand where they are coming from.

There are certain styles of communication that must be known as they affect the outcome of any conversation. They include;

- *Passive communication*: With this style, the communicator tries to avoid conflict and is more agreeable than necessary. They speak without passion and may be misunderstood because they can sometimes come across as indifferent. It is, by some people, referred to as the submissive method of communication. This is because passive communicators would much prefer to give in to the demands of others just to avoid confrontational or conflict situations. You will also find them being very apologetic people, even when they are clearly in the right.

- *Manipulative communication*: Manipulators like to choose and time their words with care. They are cunning, deceptive, and may seek to cause harm to their partners for their own selfish benefits. But they do this so shrewdly, that they rarely ever appear to be destructive. There are usually deliberate undertones to the words they speak, which convey a different meaning than is obvious. They are also quite good at making others feel sorry for what they shouldn't and then end up acting against their better judgement.

- *Aggressive communication*: These kinds of communicators may be loud and threatening in the way they express their feelings. They make demands and the rationality or kindness of their points may be lost in the intimidating nature of their approach. The aggressive communicator might imagine themselves to be close to perfection (if not perfect) and would usually ascribe the blame for every failure in their lives to others besides themselves. They are often preoccupied with getting their way to see things from a win-win perspective. While they may appear a little similar to manipulative communicators, their methods are often brash and direct — this is opposed to the more subtle and cunning style characterized by manipulators.

- *Assertive communication*: This is often declared as the best way to converse with anyone. Especially, your partner in a relationship. This is because assertiveness is not selfish. It aims for a win-win. Assertive communicators try to explain and discuss their feelings, hurt or not, without blaming their partners. Those who are assertive try to do the best they can for people but are never hesitant to say no when they need to. They can be empathetic but will also speak about their own emotions and needs without shame. They take responsibility for the results they experience, whether positive or negative, and will often look straight at whoever they are speaking with.

- *Passive-aggressive communication*: An analogy for this is anger bottled up and labeled with a smiley face. Such communicators may act unconcerned and lackadaisical, but one can often tell that they are steaming beneath the surface. Their body language and the expressions on their face with these kinds of communicators should not be trusted as an accurate picture of their true emotions. The silent treatment is the most common method used by passive-aggressive communicators.

Couples Therapy

If your partner has been on your case for a while to see a therapist about the ineffective or non-existent communication in your relationship, you should take them seriously. If they haven't, then you should suggest it to them. Whichever name you prefer to call it, therapy or counseling, the fact remains that it is one of the best and safest places to air out your relationship issues and help you learn how to listen to your partner.

Before any advice is given at all by the counselor, you can observe how they give you complete attention without interrupting or debating you while you speak. There's nothing better than having someone who is experienced at handling different kinds of relationship problems and has a balanced opinion of you and your partner, guide you through all the little (yet highly crucial) things you have missed.

Make Your Partner a Priority

Nothing else should matter when your partner is trying to share their thoughts with you. If you are too caught up in other activities to give them your full attention, then it is better to tell them and arrange a different time to have that conversation. Otherwise, you should put everything aside to listen. Quick glances to check what's going on in the kitchen or keeping up with the news update on your newspaper or the television will just show you find what your partner is sharing with you insignificant.

You should sit facing them, maintain eye contact, and catch every word and inflection as they speak. You can stop them if you missed what they had just said and would like that they repeat themselves. Otherwise, focus your mind on listening without speaking.

Think

To truly listen, you must also process what is being said. Mull it over with an open mind. Take in every word that is spoken to you ponder them. By so doing, your response will have a more positive impact on your partner.

In keeping an open mind, here are some tips to guide you;

1. Understand that people will often have differing opinions from you. You cannot always expect them to agree with you on everything. In fact, the relationship will be more enjoyable when you are with someone who is not afraid to challenge your opinions constructively and speak their mind freely. Do not see people as inferior because they express a different perspective than yours. Listen to them and try to see the reason in their opinions. Who knows, you might end up agreeing with them.

2. Don't guess what your partner is trying to say or look for deeper meaning into their words. Let them clarify themselves. This does not only include vocal speculations. You should also avoid coming to your own conclusions in your mind. If there was anything you missed while they were talking, ask that they repeat themselves. Share your understanding of all they had said to avoid misinterpretation. If certain things were not said or alluded to, don't attempt to read the mind of your partner.

3. Many times, our minds are involuntarily closed. We may have been accepting of our partner's opinions but were too distracted to even listen. Keep your focus on your partner. Otherwise, you might end up with all the wrong conclusions after you have missed some vital points of the conversation.

4. Try not to let biases of any kind color your vision of your partner. They are human beings like yourself with personal opinions, flaws, and so on. For some closed-minded people in relationships, the problem is that they think their partner's opinions are without substance and entirely reliant on what

religion they subscribe to or the popular opinion on a particular topic. Give people the benefit of the doubt. If you must make any assumptions about your partner's viewpoint, let it be that it is unbiased, rational, and intelligent.

Some benefits of open-mindedness are;

1. People will return the favor and listen to you. What is the point of having smart and helpful things to say, if no one will pay you any mind? Granted, some folks may continue to be closed-minded. But, for the most part, you would have more active listeners.

2. Your life would flourish. This is common for people who remain open to new ideas and opportunities. They have a better chance at success. This is because of the growth that comes with being open-minded. It is said that one's best assets are the people in their lives. Individuals who do not immediately shoot down others who share different opinions from them tend to have more friends and people who easily rely on and turn to them.

3. Open-mindedness would make for a fun person to be around. People would be comfortable to share their thoughts with you and you would have a lot more to say in your conversations. You add to your knowledge bank every time you take in a point of view that is new to you. Open-mindedness also tends to lead to the development of other fine qualities. Such qualities include ingenuity and originality.

4. A closed-minded person may shy away from new challenges. By so doing, they would lack the necessary confidence needed to thrive in trying situations. Usually, they look for a comfortable or familiar way to go about things and stick to it even when more effective methods are presented to them. They do not explore or push the boundaries of their potential and thus, do not grow.

5. There is a definite association between open-mindedness and creativity. People who are closed-minded about any subject will, very likely, not question their previously held beliefs on it. As such, you will find that many of these people are neither dreamers nor explorers; two hallmarks of a creative person. The open-minded individual learns the possibilities in new ideas and is not afraid to give them a try if the positives

outweigh the negatives. According to Walt Disney, you must first be able to imagine a thing before you can set out to create it. And what chance has the imagination to fly when the mind is closed shut?

Respect

If you already hold little regard for your partner, their opinions would have an even smaller stature, and it isn't much of an incentive to spend time listening to opinions you feel have no importance or are beneath you. This is why ideas like love at first sight or a whirlwind romance is not a good enough basis for any relationship. For such unions to survive the usual hurdles that are often faced by romantic relationships, both parties must have mutual respect. The importance and necessity of respect are non-negotiable for couples.

If your partner has ever accused you of not showing them respect or you worry that you are being disrespected in your relationship, below are some behaviors that, when noticed, could prove that you and your partner have some work to do in your relationship, especially when it concerns the issue of respect.

- We all have those habits which cannot go with us into a relationship. They may be fine to us, but others might not be able to tolerate them for too long. Feelings of love may not be enough of an incentive to change these aspects of ourselves. The respect you have for your partner, and one that you also expect in turn, is sure to do the trick. Say you have always complained about how your partner prefers to leave their dirty clothes in a disorderly manner in the room. Should they continue to do so without making even the slightest effort towards changing, this is a sign of disrespect.

- If you notice that your partner is only partially present when you are talking to them, it could be that they have a very small opinion of you, and vice versa. In a relationship, no one involved should have to beg for attention. Both parties should be interested in each other enough to want to listen.

- How many times have you caught your partner lying to you and then forgave them, only for that person to do it again and again? While they might try to paint it as a good thing, saying that they tell you lies to save the relationship or because they love and respect you, this is not a fact. When one is honest with their partner and works on changing certain things about themselves to avoid lying in the future, these are definite signs of respect. Understandably, some people might react to the truth in a manner that suggests they would much prefer a lie. Still, you should respect yourself and the relationship enough to keep your promise of honesty.

- For any healthy relationship to prosper, both parties must set their boundaries at the onset. It becomes the duty of both partners in the relationship to not cross the lines they had agreed to. To intentionally breach this agreement shows that the offending partner may not respect the other. It doesn't matter how ridiculous the set boundaries are or what aspects of the relationship they concern, what is important is that you and your partner agreed to them.

- While this may be a fear of commitment more than a sign of disrespect, it is possible that your partner refuses to go with you to family meetings because they have little or no respect for you. That is, they don't care about how important it is to you that they meet your family. You should ask them about this. Making a relationship work is no easy business. Sometimes, difficult sacrifices must be made. If after discussing with them, they have nothing to say as to why they don't want to meet your family, it just might be a problem of respect.

- Unless there was another agreement made by both partners, an unspoken rule of most relationships is exclusivity. As such, both partners must respect each other's feelings enough to not kiss, fondle, sext, or make love to other people. It is no secret the things that are forbidden in exclusive relationships. To do them anyway is disrespectful and can be really hurtful.

- If your partner's feelings count for nothing with you, then you will not think much about making hurtful jokes at their expense, especially in public. You should be on their side rooting for and defending them. Granted, we all make mistakes and might do things to offend our partners. But if you do not feel sorry for your actions, or if your partner does not apologize to you, then you need no other sign to recognize this blatant lack of respect.

Bad Listening Habits

There are certain habits that are common in many people which prevent us from truly listening when we are spoken to. One of them is rehearsing your reply. This may happen when you believe you know what your partner is getting at and are only waiting for them to stop talking. Another is a stubborn conviction that you are right. In such situations, it matters very little what is said as it will unlikely change your mind. Your mind would shut out all rationality. Have you ever found yourself daydreaming while someone is speaking to you? It happens more often than you think. It further stresses the point that listening is conscious and deliberate. You must make an effort to keep your mind in the here and now.

Eye Contact

Look directly at your partner while they are speaking. This is not to say that you must stare uncomfortably into their eyes without once changing your focus. But, frequently maintaining eye contact and consciously looking at them shows that you are present. Even though we do not mean to, many of us are guilty of getting distracted when our partners need our attention most. Your partner is probably not going to like you checking your social media messages at the same time they are talking to you. Such behaviors might lead them to conclude that their thoughts and emotions mean little or nothing to you.

Show That You Are Attentive

Giving your partner signs that your focus has not shifted from them may not seem like much, but it is ingrained in us to look out for proof of attentiveness when we are conversing with anyone. Nodding, repeating what was heard, and ah-hahs are some proofs that you are present in the conversation. When you do these, your partner is encouraged to relax and continue speaking. Their confidence that they are being heard is reinforced, and they appreciate you more for it. Besides occasionally repeating some of what your partner said, you may summarize all their thoughts back to them to ensure you heard right and assure your partner that they haven't just wasted their time.

CHAPTER 4

The Why And How Of Empathy

It's arguably the most important piece of a relationship, but what is empathy exactly? It's understanding the feelings of another person. In this chapter, we'll go through the different kinds of empathy, why it's so important to a romantic relationship, and how to be more empathetic. When it comes to communication, empathy is absolutely essential, so be sure to spend some time reading this chapter and thinking about your own state of empathy.

The forms of empathy

There are actually three kinds of empathy, according to experts. They are all important for building strong relationships. They are:

Cognitive empathy

This type of empathy is an awareness of what someone else is thinking and where they come from. It's usually a more intentional and conscious act as you try to take the other person's perspective. Let's say your partner has lost their job, and they are very upset. You, however, know that the job was a huge source of stress, so you know this will ultimately be a good thing. This would be a bad thing to say to your partner right now, so you can use cognitive empathy to better understand their perspective. You listen and pay attention to the feelings your partner is expressing. You imagine yourself in their position, and understand that, yes, while this turn of events may be good in the long run, right now, there's a lot of pain and frustration.

Emotional empathy (or affective empathy)

This type of empathy goes a bit further than cognitive empathy. Instead of just understanding a person's emotions, you actually *feel* them. A really good example is this is what happens when someone with strong emotional empathy sees another person crying. They don't know why this person is sad, but their immediate response is to want to cry, too. Using the lost-job example from above, your partner comes home, in tears, and while you don't know right away that it's because they've lost their job, you instantly feel sadness, too. Tears start welling up in your eyes. Emotional or affective empathy is what makes a person match someone else's emotional state. It can be overwhelming and not always helpful. You both might end up paralyzed by your emotions. Empaths, or people with a seemingly supernatural ability to feel others' emotions, have very high levels of this emotional empathy.

Empathic concern (or compassionate empathy)

For a strong, healthy relationship, the two types of empathy we've talked about so far should result in empathic concern. It's basically a combination of the two previous types into something that builds good relationships. Empathic concern is what drives a person to actually *help,* if they can. You understand why your partner is feeling upset about their lost job, you feel their sadness, and now you want to make them feel better. You won't always be certain about what to do. By using your emotional intelligence to assess the situation, and even just asking your partner what they need, you can figure it out.

Why empathy matters

It's pretty clear why empathy matters. Every person is different and responds in their own unique way to what happens around them. To communicate a sense of understanding and unity, a bridge needs to be built between people. The bridge is empathy. If you or your partner doesn't feel like they can rely on the other for understanding, compassion, and support, what's the point? The relationship will be a source of pain and stress, and not comfort.

All types of empathy are important for a relationship. Let's look at cognitive empathy first. Imagine you are the one who lost your job, and you come home to your partner. They immediately say, "Well, you hated that job, so isn't this a good thing?" You try to explain why you aren't feeling that way right now, but they just look confused. You feel like they aren't trying to see things from your perspective at all, and it's extremely frustrating.

Let's turn to emotional empathy now. You are crying, tears running down your face. Imagine that your partner is just sitting there, completely dry-eyed. Sure, you didn't expect them to burst out weeping, but they seem so at ease. Their body is rigid, and they even seem distracted by something else. Your partner failing to match your emotional state makes you feel really awkward and alone. Even though they're sitting next to you, you're on completely different planes emotionally, and it's lonely.

If your partner isn't expressing cognitive or emotional empathy, they probably won't express much empathic concern either, or at least, that's how you'll feel. Failing to see things from your perspective or feel any of your emotions makes you believe they just don't care. They aren't feeling a need to comfort you or make you feel better. This lack of empathy is essentially a lack of emotional communication that goes deeper than just words. It's a lack of soul communication. If it's a persistent problem, it will drive a wedge further and further between you and your partner. Without emotional intimacy, a relationship won't make either person happy. It will break down.

How to be more empathetic

Empathy is an innate human trait. Only certain people - like narcissists and sociopaths - don't feel empathy or relate to the feelings of others. They can sometimes fake it, even very well, but it isn't natural. Let's assume you and your partner fall into the vast majority of people who can feel empathy. It's something that can be nurtured and strengthened. It's also something you can learn to express more clearly. How do you do it?

Be intentional about putting yourself in your partner's shoes

You'll hear empathy described frequently as "walking in another person's shoes," and that's a true statement, but kind of vague. It has to be an intentional act for most people. To do it, you have to *decide* that's what you're going to do, so your other tendencies (such as giving advice right away) don't take over. As your partner talks, listen and imagine that you're the one going through the situation they're describing, or feeling the things they're feeling. You may worry that this is selfish, since you're technically thinking about you and not them, but it's the first to building empathy.

Don't judge

Feeling judged is one of the worst feelings in the world. When you believe someone is judging you, it triggers emotions like shame, guilt, bitterness, anger, and more. To build empathy between you and your partner, you want a judgment-free zone. Pay attention to the critic living in your head, and when you feel it rearing its ugly head towards your partner, don't let it speak out. Not voicing your judgments is the first step to not having them at all. Your partner will feel much safer and more comfortable being vulnerable. Next, you need to assess *why* you feel judgmental thoughts. You might be making assumptions about your partner's frame of mind when they make certain decisions or say certain things. Maybe your judgment is rooted in your own feelings of shame. When you're able to see your partner with grace and patience, you'll feel a lot more connected to them and more empathetic.

Ask questions

It can be very hard to read your partner's emotions, especially if they aren't naturally expressive. This doesn't mean empathy is impossible, however; you may just have to talk to them about their feelings. Asking questions shows that you're thinking of them and that you care about their thoughts and emotions. If you notice your partner acting a bit off in some way, don't leave them to stew by themselves. Ask them what's wrong. Even if they don't want to talk about it that second, they'll feel better knowing you noticed and that you want to help. If they do feel like talking, ask follow-up questions to get a better sense of their thought process and where their emotions are coming from. It's helpful to you, and it can be good for your partner too, since verbalizing emotions is a great way to clarify them.

Help out in concrete ways, like doing chores

Showing your partner you care by helping with chores or other responsibilities is very good for the relationship. If your partner had a bad day, let them relax and unwind while you take care of dinner. These types of actions show that you understand their emotions and are willing to make things easier for them, even if it's just in small ways. You aren't expecting them to just "shake it off" and move along with life as normal. Instead, your concrete actions let your partner know their emotions are valid, and you want to respect them. By doing a task or chore they usually do, you are showing that you're willing to literally "walk in their shoes."

Read more

This may seem like an odd way to build empathy, but the science holds up. A few years ago, two psychologists conducted a test where participants read both popular fiction and literary fiction. Literary fiction, which emphasizes characters instead of plot, gave readers a glimpse into more complex thoughts and emotions. Things aren't always spelled out in literary fiction, so a reader is prompted to exercise their emotional intelligence. Like working out a muscle, this strengthens a person's overall emotional intelligence and applies to the real world. You can also improve your empathy by seeking out books (fiction and nonfiction) by authors that are different than you. Reading perspectives from someone with a different value system, race, background, and so on helps you practice empathy.

Literary fiction examples:

The Goldfinch by Donna Tartt
The Life of Pi by Yann Martel
The Kite Runner by Khaled Hosseini
Middlesex by Jeffrey Eugenides
Little Fires Everywhere by Celeste Ng
Lincoln in the Bardo by George Saunders

Communicating During Conflict

Conflicts are part of every romantic relationship, even healthy ones. In fact, no conflict at all is usually a sign that one or both people in the couple aren't communicating their true feelings. They want to avoid the common downfalls of arguing, like shouting or insults or hurt feelings, so they choose to stay quiet. However, this forces bad feelings to simmer and spread, brewing up resentment and bitterness. The solution is to express instead of hoard. But how can a couple do that without things escalating?

Where communicating during conflict usually goes wrong

When engaging in a conflict, there are a handful of ways where things usually go wrong. It never hurts to review them, though, and there are some issues we haven't gotten into yet:

Someone gets defensive

When arguing, getting sensitive and defensive is never an effective way to communicate. It's a way to deflect blame and not address the actual problem your partner is trying to bring up. It also pits you against your partner; you feel they are attacking you. With this mindset, actual change and resolution is very difficult. If this is a common occurrence in your relationship, both you and your partner (regardless of who tends to get defensive) will probably avoid bringing anything contentious up in conversations.

The argument is always something to be "won"

Most people make the mistake of going into conflicts believing there will be a "winner" and a "loser." The problem with this mindset is that it establishes a me vs. you dynamic. Instead of working together as a team to find a solution, you and your partner are enemies. You don't want to compromise or give ground, because that means you're "losing." Going into arguments like this actually sets you both up for failure and nobody ends up happy.

You and your partner make assumptions about the other person

Making assumptions and believing you know what your partner is thinking and feeling rarely works out, especially in arguments. In the heat of the moment, you are more likely to assume negative things about your partner, and react in anger and frustration. A lot of arguments are actually misunderstandings taken to an aggressive level. Nobody gets the chance to really express what they mean and feel, and even if things eventually become clear, feelings have already been hurt.

You aren't actually listening to each other

When tensions are high and you're arguing with your partner, it's very easy to get stuck inside your own head. You're feeling a lot of emotions, probably negative ones, and maybe making a lot of assumptions about your partner's thought process. This is all distracting you from what your partner is actually saying to you. You might hear their voice, but you aren't really *listening*. Any conversion without real listening, including an argument, isn't productive or helpful.

How to improve communication during conflict

You know the mistakes couples tend to make during arguments, and maybe you recognize them in your own relationship. What can be done to improve communication during arguments and conflicts?

Be more empathic

Putting yourself in your partner's shoes helps strip away the me vs. you mindset and can make compromise easier.

Clearly state what you're feeling

A lot of arguments break down because neither person in the relationship will just say what they're feeling. There's a lot of "you" statements and not enough "I" statements. You need to let your partner know how you're feeling about things in a clear way, so they aren't stuck with a bunch of assumptions or frustrations because they can't read your mind. If you are feeling upset or hurt by something they've done or said, simply say, "I'm feeling hurt and upset by this."

Be kind

This fits into being more empathic, but since empathy can be tricky for a lot of people, it might be easier to just remember to be kind to your partner during an argument. Don't resort to insults, name-calling, or any other intentional hurtful action. This could include strong physical reactions, like waving your arms around or throwing/punching inanimate objects. While you might never dream of hurting your partner physically, unpredictable physical reactions can still make a conflict very scary, and depending on your partner's past, it could trigger them.

Even during the most difficult conflicts, your partner is still a human being and deserves to be treated with respect. You deserve the same in return, so if you feel that your partner is being unkind to you during an argument, let them know. Remember to use "I" statements, such as, "I feel really hurt when you use that tone/call me that name/etc."

Be a more active listener

As we said earlier, not listening is a big reason why arguments become ineffective and hurtful. To improve communication, commit to more active listening. Instead of trying to think of what you're going to say next while you're partner is talking, actually pay attention to their words. Don't interrupt them before they're finished. Active listening can prevent a lot of misunderstandings and ensures both people in the argument feel understood.

Be willing to take responsibility

Taking responsibility for things that harm the relationship is the opposite of being defensive. Rather than trying to deflect blame, actually think about what your partner is saying, and own what you're responsible for. This is what a mature person does. They are willing to say, "Yeah, I messed up," and move forward to finding a solution. This will really help your partner's ability to be vulnerable with you. They know that instead of making excuses or getting defensive, you are willing to own up to your mistakes.

Always be looking for compromise

Most conflicts have a compromise. We say "most," because there are some things a couple might decide are deal-breakers, but that's up to each individual. In general, every argument has a solution that both people can be happy with. While engaged in conflict, always be on the lookout for that solution. This accomplish this, you can't see arguments as something to be won or lost. Your ultimate goal will be a peaceful resolution with two happy people.

Take a timeout if necessary

Sometimes arguments escalate to the point where nothing can settle it down except some time apart. Maybe you're both yelling at each other and emotions are just too overwhelming. That's okay. It isn't the end of the world. The best solution at this point is for both people to take a timeout to cool down. A walk or shower or even a good night's sleep can help reset you and your partner's emotions, and give you some perspective. It is a good idea to let your partner know that's what your plan is, and that you do plan on returning to the conversation.

CHAPTER 5

The Importance of Work On Yourself First

The couple is made of two people; both must be responsible for their balance first. Change yourself to the better if you want to help your partner to be a better person.

Everybody gets angry for one reason or the other. Whether it shows or not, we are all bound to feeling tension when people overstep their boundaries, or certain matters go wrong. In marriages, spouses can avoid showing anger to avoid conflict. They shove it down and let it go unnoticed.

However, hidden anger is just as bad as that which explodes because, at one point or the other, it will hurt the relationship. In most cases, the more one lets the arguments to go on, the more the distance between him/her and the partner grows. The longer it lasts, the harder it is for the couple to repair the relationship and at such points, people look for divorce papers.

As human beings, anger pushes us to say or do things that WE would not do in normal circumstances. We should remember that once words are said and actions are done, it is impossible to unsay or undo them. When we explode, we should be careful about how we deal with anger. The emotion of anger is not right or wrong by itself. The morality of emotions and feelings comes in question only when we react to what we are feeling. For example, feeling angry is okay but destroying things out of anger brings the morality aspect.

Causes of conflicts between couples

More often than not, human beings forget that they are different and that each has a different opinion and view of things. This happens a lot in marriage because the love and attraction make the couple feel like they are one. Although marriage brings 'two people together to become one' their minds still differ, their backgrounds are different, their upbringing is different; therefore they cannot have the same opinions all the time.

Everyone has a different memory and perception, and there is no one right and standard way of thinking. Even when you know that your opinion is right, your line of thought and perspective is not the only right one. A couple consists of two people, and if it is only one person who keeps giving their opinion without considering the opinion of the other one, then the marriage is made up on one person. This means that there is no room in the marriage for the two people and thus the communication stops, and the marriage no longer functions properly.

There are many different ways of dealing with issues positively without having fights that will end up destroying the communication. Spouses do not have to strive to fix each other rather; they should look for ways to agree and disagree positively. A couple should constantly deal with unresolved anger and issues. Do not bottle up things, feelings, emotions, opinions et cetera even if it is for the sake of the other person. Letting thing go without sorting them out fast and soon only leads to deeper conflicts and more distance to the extent of everyone using a confrontational tone and attitude even when they should not.

How to deal with anger

Firstly, when a spouse is wrong, he/she should not hesitate to apologize. Words such as 'I am sorry' go a long way in making a partner reconsider their next words. When honesty is applied by the person apologizing, there is no more room for more arguments. Conceding defeat does not make one weak and apologizing helps to loosen tension which might have escalated to disconnection and complete lack of communication. Staying stubborn and trying to 'fix' a partner will not help solve anything. Standing a ground is only necessary when the couple will win together but if the victory belongs to one person, chances are a brick wall will grow between them. It is therefore important that everybody communicates effectively, practice saying the right things to each other, build one another, talk to each other and avoid talking at one another.

Communication as a cornerstone to work on yourself

If one were to go to a crowd of people and ask them to name the most important aspect of marriage, they would mention a variety of things including trust, honesty love et cetera. Every person has their understanding of love and marriage, and they have their preferences. Of course, all the aspects that the people would mention play a crucial role in marriages but communication is the centerpiece of all communication.

The way the two spouses communicate with each other, discuss their issues, encourage and build one another through communication is essential for the sustainment of a fulfilling marriage. One can say that communication is the vehicle that carries all the other aspects of marriage. Without communication, that is verbal and verbal; a spouse could not know whether to trust and be honest with their partners. Assumptions usually break the marriage. If one person loves the other and does not talk about it or at least show it in words, they will not succeed in marriage. To the spouses; if you love your partner, let them know through words and actions.

If the communication between two people is honest, then the chances of the relationship surviving are high. Communication is the cornerstone of all relationship; however, many people are not good at communicating. Other people do not know how to address matters in the right way. Spouses need to use certain communication channels to create a strong and caring atmosphere in their marriage. Love, honesty trust and other important parts of marriage are not meaningful by themselves. One must be able to express these aspects to give them meaning. The expression of love and care in marriage is what makes it worth envy. Showing love acting honestly and showcasing trust is where the magic of marriage lies. The ability to communicate with a spouse about how much they mean to each other is where a marriage graduates from good to great. One should remember that communication is more than speaking about things; it is also showing. Under the umbrella of communication between couples, we can identify verbal, non-verbal and physical acts.

Verbal communication between couples

Verbal communication is the easiest and most commonly used form of communication. Words are easy to use to a large extent. People like to hear things especially when they are nice. For instance, every spouse loves to be complemented through words 'you look very nice today,' 'I love you.' You are a great person with an amazing personality.' Effective communication requires one to be able to express their feelings to their spouse through words. If a couple loves each other so much yet they are unable to communicate the same through words; they might never know how much they mean to each other. Even when the actions show clearly that the spouses love one another, they still need to say it in words. Words will add value to the actions and vice versa. They will make the involved parties feel appreciated, loved, and sure about how the other person feels.

Along with all the compliments and expression of the positive, the spouses can express what they are not happy about through words. If a spouse is doing something that is offending the other, yet the offended person is silent about it, the offender will most probably continue with their habits. Silence does not help in most cases. If anything, lack of communication will keep hurting the couple. One cannot possibly go through life while holding all the dissatisfaction inside. Verbal communication will help one let it all out. However, when letting matters out, one should be tactful and careful. Care and warmth in communication are essential, especially when talking about matters that might bring disagreements. Couples should not wait too long before they say something about things bothering them. They should also not wait too long before telling each other that they care.

Nonverbal communication between couples

At some point in life, we have said something unpleasant or unfriendly to someone else. They might not have retaliated verbally, but they show their displeasure through facial expressions and actions either voluntarily or involuntarily. The offended person did not have to say a word to tell the story, but it all showed on their faces. Human beings share more with their faces and body than they would give credit.

Spouses should be aware of their facial expression and body language while talking to their partners to avoid giving off the wrong message. Human beings are capable of reading the body language of their partners even subconsciously. If for example, a couple is having a serious conversation and one person id hunched over and probably closed off, the other will detect a lack of vulnerability. Use the right facial and body language for every conversation. For example, if a couple s having a serious conversation, it is important that the two parties Face each other and keep their body language open without crossing the legs or arms. The body language should show that the person is listening keenly, taking note of the important things and is willing to work through the subject matter. Nonverbal cues are many, and they communicate to the partner either positively or negatively even without an exchange of words. Everyone should be conscious and thoughtful of how their body language brings out their thoughts.

Physical acts

Physical acts include making dinner, doing the laundry, taking out the garbage, and even getting ice-cream from the fridge for a pregnant wife. Physical actions are not things one can express through words. They are things that one does for their spouses to show them how much they care. IN DOING SUCH simple things, one is communicating with their partners about how much they mean to them without using words. This form of communication falls under the phrase "Actions speak louder than words." You could sing your spouse that you love them till your face turns blue, but it would not mean as much as making him/her dinner or replacing their old attire. The power of actions outdoes the power of saying I love you 300 times a day.

Having in mind that communication is important for the success of marriage; one cannot rely on just one of the ways mentioned above. Every spouse should strike a balance between the three to ensure that the marriage thrives. It is okay for a spouse to tell their partner that they love them and at the same time give an opinion about things that are bothering them. Open communication will benefit the marriage in the long term and become an investment to reap from. Every person should use body language to show their spouses that they are honest and open with them. An observant eye will pick negative body language no matter how well one hides it. A spouse may take this as a red flag for the beginning of the end of the marriage. Couples need to stay alert about what they communicate through their bodies and make appropriate adjustments so that the spouse can read honesty and trust

Again, a couple should use actions to communicate to their spouses A gift or two, a body massage, a dinner date, or even assisting with a troubling task can go a long way to communicate to each other. Actions will always speak for themselves; even if one was to keep singing that they love someone yet they fail to show it in actions, then they will fail. Without open and effective communication, a couple will face more challenges and obstacles than otherwise.

CHAPTER 6

Communication at the Beginning of Budding Relationships

If you take the time to open good lines of communication at the beginning of a relationship it can help you immensely as you move forward together. Of course, it goes without saying that honesty is extremely important at this time so no matter what, be honest with yourself and with your partner.

Of course, sex is generally a big part of any relationship but it is usually even more so at the beginning. While these can be some of the most difficult conversations to have, especially with a new partner, there are certain ones that you will want to have even before you have sexual relations.

Here are a few of them for you:

What type of relationship are they looking for? Friendly or romantic? Sexual or non-sexual? Committed or non-committed? Monogamous or not? If you don't match up here you may want to reconsider going any further?

When was the last time they were tested for an STD/STI? Which ones were they tested for and what were the results? How many partners have they been with since their last test? Did they use protection? This is also a good time to ask if they have ever shared a needle with someone for tattoos, drugs, or piercings because unfortunately some STI's are transmitted this way.

What about birth control? Which methods do they prefer/use? Is there any possibility of a current pregnancy? Are they open to the possibility of pregnancy? Protecting yourselves from unintended STI's or pregnancies shows that you are responsible and that you care, setting some solid groundwork for open lines of communication. And just remember that the best time to discuss safe sex is before you move to the bedroom. A really good way to start the discussion is by telling them that you truly care about them and you want to ensure that you're both protecting each other and the relationship. You may want to start by voicing your own preferences first as this may make your partner feel more comfortable with the discussion. In this day and age, it is also not a bad idea to go get tested together for mutual support.

The same goes for safer-sex. Do they utilize dental dam or other barriers? What activities do they enjoy without the use of barriers? There are all important conversations to have on this subject and should be discussed as early in the relationship as possible. It is completely natural to feel a little embarrassed bringing the subject up but both you and your partner will be glad you did. Take the guesswork out discuss it early on.

As you explore and get to know one another sexually, educate them on what kind of touch you enjoy or where and how you like to be kissed. You can and should also take this chance to set any boundaries that you are just not willing to try. Is there anywhere that you don't like being touched or kissed? Tell them now because remember, that shudder can be misinterpreted as joy and pleasure unless you articulate and let them know.

Are there activities or fantasies that you know you want to explore? Maybe there are some that you'd like to talk about or even role play or act out. Just remember to be receptive to listening to your partner's desires as well so again it is important to discuss boundaries before having this discussion to avoid making this conversation turn awkward. If you aren't comfortable discussing your fantasies you can try themed porn movies or books and share them together and when the time is right, start the conversation on it with something like, "I enjoyed the ____ scene. Maybe that's something we can try."

Something you both may find useful, and maybe even a little exciting, is making a yes/no/maybe chart. You both go off on your own and list out the things you know you enjoy (Yes), ones you don't like or are not willing to try (No), and then the one you might be interested in. Once complete then share your lists with each other and perhaps flip a coin to see who gets to have one of their Yeses used tonight. This can open some wonderful door for communication and also give you some revealing insight on one another.

Many people learn what they like and don't like by having sex with a partner while others utilize masturbation to get to know their bodies. When you learn how to give yourself orgasms it can make it easier to do so with a partner. Do you like it fast or slow? How much pressure feels good? What makes you uncomfortable? Once you know how to please yourself it is much easier to be able to show your partner how to touch you. You can also crank this up a notch by masturbating in front of each other so you can show them exactly how and then work it into mutual masturbation and take it slow, talk to each other and verbalize clearly when they do something right or wrong.

While talking about sex can be a little awkward or even scary, it can also be very eye-opening and even a turn-on. You can always start the conversation about sex by directly asking them what feels good or what kind of bedroom fun they are interested in. And then you can follow-up by letting them know what feels good to you or what you are wanting to try.

Communication in the Marriage

Having that two-way street open line of communication is a must-have for any marriage to be successful. Many divorces could be turned around if the spouses simply improved the ways in which they communicate. Simple bad habits are often the ones that get couples into trouble and once the marriage detours onto a rough road, it is very easy for negativity to grow. From there it is easy for the problems to escalate as the couple repeats the same mistakes over and over. However, some of those bad habits and simple communication mistakes can be easily be resolved with just a little effort.

Yelling

Many times, when we are angry we immediately start to raise our voice, sometimes just to release or express the tension of the situation. All too often we end up causing more tension and trouble because we take the easy option of yelling at each other. While releasing this tension by yelling may feel satisfying, it is usually short-lived because what we say in anger can sometimes be hurtful and is likely to escalate the argument.

We release a lot of negative emotions when we yell and from that point forward it can be extremely difficult to communicate. Those emotions will overshadow everything else that you are trying to discuss because the negativity will be what captures your partner's attention the most. And because you have now set them up to be defensive as opposed to being an understanding and responsive, they will likely miss the other points of your conversation or may even misunderstand the entire reason for the discussion in the first place.

Yelling immediately sets the groundwork for a heated exchange of emotions rather than open communication. Emotional exchanges can easily divert into an extremely destructive habit and we have to change so that we are communicating in a way that lets us voice our feelings, frustrations, and emotions so that we can move past them together. For our message to be clear, we have to learn to keep our emotions and check.

If you find that emotions are getting too heated a great way to reduce the stress and distract you from the hot emotions is to take a break from the conversation for a 15-minute workout. It is kind of hard to remain angry or to focus on anything other than yourself when you're trying to catch your breath and all of the good endorphins can actually help calm you down.

And of course, if you detect the conversation detouring into a yelling match you can always use that pause button. Take 15 to 30 minutes away from each other and go do something you enjoy such as watching TV, or reading a magazine or book or even taking a shower or bath. This will give you both time to calm down and to think about how you want to approach the discussion. You'll find that you can get through problems together a lot more easily if you are on each other side instead of pushing each other away.

Name Calling

In the same way that our voice can rise with our temper, our vocabulary can devolve very rapidly. While pet names can be cute and endearing, words do hurt and may cause irreparable damage if we resort to name-calling during an argument. While it may seem appropriate at the time and movies and TV shows like to focus and poke fun at name-calling during arguments, hitting someone with a dirty or inappropriate name during the heat of an argument can have more sting than a physical strike. It can be exceedingly difficult to forgive someone when they stoop to this level and sometimes the hurt can last for days or even longer. Unfortunately, sometimes resulting in the breakup of the relationship.

Once you tear into that can of worms it leaves you open for a return volley and you just might not like what you hear back. This can end up diluting the issue and lead you both into a shouting match filled with hurtful names that neither of you will be able to take back. Again, this is why it is important to take a step back or to use that pause button when we detect that tempers are flaring. Don't say something that you're going to regret. Think before you speak.

When It's ALL about "I" And Not "Us."

While it is important that we began many conversations utilizing the "I" starters, we have to remember that the central focus of a marriage must come back to "us." Take a look at your regular day-to-day conversations that you have with your spouse and see if you see behaviors that may need to change. Do they seem to revolve around your mood, day, plans, or what you expect from your spouse? If so then you may want to start peppering your conversations with questions about your partner's plans/mood/etc. to help even out your daily interactions.

Do small little things throughout the day that let your partner know you're thinking about them. Whether with a flirty text or a quick call just to say hello, when you communicate for no other reason than to communicate our love or affection it helps solidify the building blocks for that two-way street of communication.

Try to be more thoughtful, considerate, and generous toward your spouse and they are likely to reciprocate. Try to surprise them by knocking out one of their chores for them or by planning a special meal that you know they truly enjoy. If you focus on improving in these areas and keep it consistent, your spouse will eventually say or do something in kind. These kinds of behaviors can really help strengthen the foundation and nurture a great marriage.

Of course, old habits are hard to break and it will take some practice to break some of these common communication mistakes but it can be amazing how just a few small changes can change the energy of a marriage. If at first, you don't see your spouse reciprocating, don't give up. At first, it is easy to want to give up if they haven't seemed to notice but if you keep going you'll find that the more you act with generosity, the more loving and generous you feel toward your spouse.

Competitive Attitudes in Marriage

Everybody likes to win and many of us are competitive by nature but while we may strive to be the top dog or to stay ahead in many areas of our lives, our marriages should not be one of. If one of you is always the winner, both of you lose. If you try to win every argument every time you may end up hurting or even demoralizing your partner more so than anything else.

Stop and think about why you feel the need to always win. Sometimes emotional insecurities can cause us to overcompensate by trying to look superior to our spouses. If we stay on top it is easier to feel stronger and more confident but having the weight of us constantly over them can actually make them feel insecure. Remember, communicating is not about being right or winning but about working as a team. If you find yourself mentally making bullet points for every disagreement for you to make your point or to win the argument you could end up doing a lot more harm than good.

Never Wrong

Whether you admit it or not, you are not perfect and you will make mistakes. While it can sometimes be hard to admit when we're wrong if we want to have a strong relationship there are going to be times when we have to apologize or admit that we were wrong. Don't be afraid of showing weakness by admitting you're wrong. That kind of stuff is for teenagers. If you try to "always be right" or try to deny or rationalize your behavior then your relationship will turn unhealthy fast. "I'm sorry" and "I was wrong" are all too underused in relationships but can go a long way toward building a better relationship.

Communication through Hardships

Unfortunately, life tends to throw many hurdles, obstacles, and curveballs in our way, and in any relationship, it can be difficult to communicate effectively during these hard times. Whether it's a new baby, new job, relocation, or financial difficulties the reality is that all couples eventually face tough times. It usually is very painful to be in a situation where you have no control and unfortunately some people just aren't able to get back up on their own when life knocks them off their feet and they need a little help.

This is especially true when it comes to relationships. If one person is feeling overwhelmed by the trials and tribulations and they do not feel supported can communicate, it can deteriorate the marriage quickly. This is why building strong two-way communication is so vital early on in the relationship, you have to be able to discuss the sometimes embarrassing hardships and face them together.

In a healthy relationship, we can never deny, minimize, or disregard the problem at hand when we are faced with a challenging situation. We must acknowledge situations and work together toward a resolution. Your active listening skills and just being there for your spouse when they need you are two of the biggest things you can utilize to help see you through the hard times.

One place that may sound strange to start is by sitting down together and discussing other bad times you have both experienced, whether together or separately. The reason for this is to show yourself and each other that you've faced tough times in the past and were able to get through them. Most of us are usually convinced that this current hardship is the worst experience of our life but when we stop to think about all the times we were able to get through other life-changing events it can actually make us feel stronger and more confident facing this one together.

Stressful situations can be overwhelming, but if we let the conversation become overheated, it can be nearly impossible for either of you to make a rational decision. While it is true that running away from your problems never helps, that doesn't mean that you can't hit that pause button that we've discussed too much. This is where it becomes really important to remove yourselves from the situation, and the conversation, long enough to give you both time to think clearly and more rationally. However, it doesn't mean that you have to ingrain yourselves so deeply into the issue that you end up with blinders on to the other aspects of your life.

If you find that you just can't seem to have a discussion on the topic without it turning heated, then it may be useful to fall back on some of the other techniques we've discussed. One of the better ones that I have found for these difficult situations is to utilize letter writing. Don't use text. Text can feel too impersonal and it will seem more from the heart if it is a handwritten letter. Remember to keep emotion out of it, make it concise, and ensure that you list every key area needing to be discussed and any ideas that you have for resolving the current hardship. After this initial discussion, you may want to take a break to give your partner the opportunity to respond back with their own letter to forgo any defensiveness.

In any relationship, there can come a time when we have to make the choice to forgive. No matter what the reason is for our resentment or anger we are going to have to let it go if the relationship has any hope of survival. We have to make the decision to accept what happened and no longer hold it against our partner. This will let you move forward because you are no longer focusing on the negative feelings and thoughts.

As we discussed, relationships are built on trust and without it, they will die, dry up, and blow away. We can easily start to build trust when we are reliable and follow through on even the little things in our daily lives. This makes the hardships so much easier to deal with because your partner will feel safe and secure knowing that you will do what needs to be done and what you say you'll do. Consistently keeping your promises is one sure way to build your partner's trust.

The same goes if you find yourself trying to regain trust. Breaking someone's trust can be a very difficult hardship to overcome and unfortunately, many relationships do not survive it. Following through and keeping your promises on little things can show your spouse that you are serious and can be trusted to keep your word. While I never recommend being untruthful or untrustworthy in any relationship, as we all know it, unfortunately, happens all too often. No matter the reason for the break in trust it can be almost an impossible pill to swallow and it will take time, energy, and work to rebuild it back to the levels you desire.

Relationships are priceless but require a lot of work and energy. Many spouses neglect to put energy into their relationship and expect it to work out on its own and they forget to make their spouse feel special, appreciated, and sometimes even loved. If you want to keep the relationship thriving you must actively pursue each other throughout the relationship. This includes both through the good times and the bad. Putting energy into the relationship can be even more important during the hardships and simply holding hands, looking into each other's eyes while you speak, or just setting aside time for just the two of you can communicate to your partner that you truly do care. The current issue at hand may affect the other aspects of your lives but it doesn't have to have a negative effect on the relationship. Actively pursuing your partner through the hardships helps affirm that you are on the same team and that together you can conquer anything.

Patience is a virtue that will come in quite handy throughout the relationship but even more so as you face hardships together. Don't let the hardship damage your relationship. Stay away from sarcasm, lecturing, swearing, and name-calling and realize that if you are not careful the hardship can indeed adversely affect you and your loved one's relationship. You will find that things work out so much better when you turn toward your partner instead of away from them.

Work together and shift gears in your mindset. Stop thinking "poor us" or focusing solely on one fix to the issue. Actively pursue other strategies and ask for your partner's input. What are some other ways to resolve the current hardship? How can you learn from this situation? How can you use it to grow closer together?

Breaking up your routine can be fun at any time in a relationship, but it can be extremely helpful during those tough times. Get out together and try something new even if it's just taking a drive, going for a stroll, or trying a new restaurant it can help alleviate the negative pressure on you and bring you closer together by helping keep those lines of communication open.

Never try to assign blame even when blame is warranted. Pointing fingers will never help the situation and we have to remember that everyone makes mistakes. For a healthy relationship we have to forgive but of course, this doesn't mean that you're condoning the behavior or actions of the current situation. You are just working together to move past it.

It may be easier for you to view hardships like climbing a huge mountain and use these five steps to help get you through:

- Bring supplies - find activities that energize you and your partner. It will take quite a bit of an effort to get over this mountain.

- Create a map - consider each of your concerns, what you would like to accomplish, and how you think you should get there.

- Bring a compass - this is simply setting benchmarks to let you see your progress up the mountain.

- Break up the duties - create a plan that lays out exactly what each of you will do to resolve the situation. It may be helpful to set a specific timetable for each of the duties to be completed and in what order they should be attacked. This doesn't mean that you cannot work together, it's just to help lighten the workload for you both. This is also a good place to schedule some time for you two to be alone. Think of it as a base camp. Don't get hung up on the issue and set some time aside for some quality time.

- Get an aerial view - set aside specific time to discuss the situation, your concerns, and how it is affecting you. Listen to each other and thoroughly take into consideration any ideas that are brought forth. Comfort each other. Take the time to keep each other warm and to keep the other from falling off the ledge. It is usually only going to be you two at the summit and you need to work together to keep each other safe and happy.

Whether or not the outcome of your choices proved to be effective or not, there always comes the time that we have to accept them and move forward. Be sure to take a moment to thank each other for the parts played getting through the hardship together. Don't think about who did what or who didn't do something, focus on the positives and move forward.

To move forward together we must have those open lines of communication. Don't dwell on the past or coulda/woulda/shoulda's and move forward together using it as a learning experience and strengthening your relationship together. Strong relationships take a lot of work and don't just happen overnight and having that two-way street of communication can help you make your relationship strong and long-lasting.

CHAPTER 7

Approaching a Group for Rapport Building

Yes, you can make good friends just about anywhere. Even if you are in an unknown place where you don't know anyone or in a new city! Chatting up with unknown people is a great way to grow your social circle and make new friends. The ability to approach a group already involved in the discussion is a huge plus because this can target many people for interaction at once.

If you are anything like I was in the days when I'd just started working, you are petrified of groups. You find the task of approaching a group highly daunting and intimidating. Being nervous is alright. It requires slightly intermediate or advanced communication skills to be able to earn a breakthrough in a group. However, it isn't impossible. It is pretty doable.

Each time I approached a group, it would feel like I am entering a den filled with hungry lions. As soon as you walk towards the groups and start speaking, there is a tremendous amount of pressure to say and do the right things. Everyone has their gaze fixed on you, and you better make it worth their while by saying or doing something interesting. Otherwise, you are just another unwanted intrusion.

It is precisely for this reason that people are wary of approaching groups. They will only begin conversations with people appear to be by themselves (much easier). However, this limits your options of connecting with maximum people, making more friends and revamping your social circle. People who've mastered the art of approaching groups smoothly and effortlessly are stars at any party. They will skillfully glide from one group to another. Others can't find the courage to do it until they've downed a couple of drinks. However, you can be a successful communicator who can approach any group with practice and effort wherever you are currently in your social confidence level.

Here are some of the best tips that can help you slay it like a boss when it comes to communicating with a bunch of people you are approaching or meeting for the first time.

Dynamics and Tips for Approaching and Communicating With Groups

I am going to share some of my best secrets that will make sure that your first few moments of interaction with the group are effortlessly killer. Instead of accumulating a bunch of cold shoulders are icy stares, you'll make more friends.

It is easier to approach a group of people in some places over others. By their nature bars, clubs, cafes, and pubs are easy places to approach a group huddled under one roof to let their hair down and enjoy. Being chatty, interesting and approaching new people here is part of the territory, so people won't really look at you like you've landed straight from Mars if you approach them in any of these places. Start with these places if you are overwhelmed by the idea of approaching groups already engaged in a conversation. The atmosphere is more relaxed, and people more or less expect to be approached by strangers.

Now, there are other places which are may be informal and relaxed, but people aren't exactly squeezed together here. For instance, a tourist favorite beach. These are people are huddled with their own intimate circle pretty much oblivious to people around them.

It's a challenge to communicate with groups where you don't know their purpose for being in a particular place. For example, a group sitting in an isolated park. Are they receptive to a rank stranger infiltrating their intimate gathering? The most awkward part is people seeing and staring at you all the way while you walk up to them, which hampers your ability to approach them smoothly. Leave these for later when you've developed sufficient confidence in approaching people in a more 'watering hole,' friendly type of places where approaching strangers and groups is a norm.

Here are some tips to approach groups like a pro

1. Avoid starting off with a closed-ended question – Once you introduce yourself and initiate conversation with a group that's already involved in a discussion (wait until they finish speaking), don't start off with a closed-ended question. Chances are these strangers who aren't too familiar with you will simply answer the question in a word or two and keep quiet again. Then there's an awkward silence. Since you approached the group in the first place, the onus of picking up the conversation falls back on you. The most likely outcome of asking a closed-ended question is you'll hang around for some time before leaving. Initially, people may answer your question to avoid coming across as impolite. However, eventually, you'll be left with no option but to quit.

Instead, assume responsibility by demonstrating proactiveness right from the beginning. Don't use questions that can be answered in a word or two to begin the conversation. You'll have to fight for conversation after the question is answered. Else, you'll have no business being in it.

The thing is, I wouldn't recommend starting a conversation with a group using a question. People are really receptive to answering questions from strangers. They feel like they aren't obliged to reply to you. Even if they do answer your question, they'll seldom expand on it. You'll be left in a situation where you will look awkward hanging around. Instead, add something of value to the group. Don't take away their time by posing questions. Unless you create more conversations from the question, avoid asking questions. Walk up to the group with something fascinating, exciting and valuable. This makes them more receptive to you.

2. Use the foot in the door strategy I often use while approaching a group. If you are slightly shy and low on confidence while approaching a large group, get your foot in the door by chatting up a person in the group. It's the same strategy we used in high school to make our way into the most popular and coolest gang. To get an entryway into the group, a majority of us would befriend someone from the group. Ina bigger group, spot a person who is on the periphery or not in the center of all the action. They appear left out or disinterested in the topic or seem focused elsewhere.

Start by approaching this person, who will most likely be receptive and open to what you are saying. Once you are able to strike a conversation with them, slowly transition your attention toward the group, while speaking to everyone. Ensure that you use this technique only on someone who doesn't appear interested in the group's talk. Don't try to switch the attention of a person who is clearly engaged and participating actively in the group conversation. You can also hold on until a group member is on their own. They may separate from the group to buy a drink or visit the restroom. This is your chance! Start talking when they are alone. Later, join their friends with them. The person will more likely than not introduce you to the group.

When it comes to professional networking or approaching a group of people at a party, gain access to the group gradually and incrementally. Unobtrusively introduce yourself to a person within the group. After a single line introduction, throw in a line about how you'd love to be introduced to the entire group at the right time. The person will more often than not oblige. "I'd really love to be introduced to your co-workers some time if you wouldn't mind."

When the person introduces you to the bigger group, come up with "it's wonderful to meet you all here" and then slip back into listening mode until you are comfortable enough to add value to the conversation. It may take time. In fact, you should take the time to understand the rhythm, flow, and nature of communication within the group. Don't try to jump in with your two cents immediately. Listen, and understand until you are confident of joining back in the conversation. When members of the group disperse or separate, there is a lull in the group conversation. Use this opportunity to strike up a conversation with the remaining group members.

If a group is already engaged in a discussion, wait for people to finish speaking before going up to them and introducing yourself. Follow this up by establishing your objective for approaching the group. For example, Hey, I am John Baker with xyz organization. How are you all? I don't want to interrupt but just wanted to listen to this rather interesting conversation since I caught a few bits of it. More often than not, people won't mind you joining the conversation unless it is something intimate or secretive, in which case you'll be politely told to back off. When it is sufficiently established that people do not want you to be a part of the group interaction, leave gracefully rather than lingering around awkwardly. Find another group that is more open and receptive.

3. The only reason why people seldom approach groups is that they imagine the worst, which is being turned away or rejected in the harshest, most humiliating manner. This isn't the case most of the times, especially if you are approaching them in a courteous, friendly and respectful manner, and not aggressively hitting on them. Generally, at worst, they'll respond in a more noncommittal manner and then get back to talking with each other leaving you on the periphery.

Now there are two ways to look at this, you get the message, and move on (which frankly no one on the outside even notices). Then there is another way, which isn't to be confused with when the group is not very open to joining you. Here, the group may be open and accepting of you joining in, but they may not make a lot of effort to involve you in the interaction simply because they expect you to make an effort or initiate yourself into the conversation. You may begin by being the silent person on the outlines. Now if you feel left out of the conversation or rejected, it is more likely your own ideas. The group will be glad to include you in the discussion of you put in more effort.

4. Don't steal anyone's thunder – Do not, I repeat, do not try one-upmanship games in a group to impress people. Avoid stealing another person's thunder if you want to gel effortlessly with the group. Make The mandatory personal introduction with ruffling feathers or sweeping the carpet from some else's feet. Establish your benign intentions, listen, respond and learn. You get a better opportunity to follow-up up with your view and create memorable and meaningful conversation.

5. Consider your position and jump in – Where do you want to position yourself in a group? Give yourself a maximum advantage, so you don't end up hanging on the periphery of the group interaction. According to communication experts, your position in the group largely determines your role in the conversation. If you are seated at the end of a table, you'll most likely feel left out of the conversation. Position yourself in the center to stay in the middle of the group interaction flow. It also subtly reinforced that you are the focal point of the discussion or central to the interaction. Being seated far doesn't make you look like a part of the interaction, which is exactly how it will be.

6. Vary your techniques according to group members – Based on the conversation, the personality of group members, the communication style of the group and so on you will have to vary your communication style. There is no one size fits all when it comes to group communication. Adapt to different groups. Mostly, a large group conversation at an informal event, party or social gathering will be more boisterous. In such a scenario, speaking softly will help you have conversations with yourself, not with others.

Even if you aren't a socially confident person, project a confident persona. Go deep, utilize your diaphragm to the fullest and articulate your words clearly, so you've heard. At times, someone may talk over you when they can't hear you. At times we may not speak with passion and conviction, which gives the other person an opportunity to cut in. Speak loudly, confidently and passionately to be heard.

Some communication experts suggest using a quieter than louder approach, especially at professional gatherings. They believe being quieter helps you get more attention than being louder. People who speak loudly may not communicate with power or authority, thus holding attention. Speak deeply in a low tone which resonates and creates the right impact. Keep your voice low pitched and impactful without demonstrating nervousness. Lower your volume, voice, and tone to express that you have something, which should be heard. Express your ideas with an element of authority. Politely and assertively prevent yourself from being interrupted.

You should be a good listener if you want to be a good group speaker. Know when to be polite, and when you need to strike. Sometimes, the only way to get your foot in the door is by interrupting. Take risks, use different strategies and practice. You won't know what works for certain types of groups and what doesn't until you practice. Use the right timing for interjecting. Keep conversations lighter in the beginning. Apologize when needed. Use humor generously to cleverly disarm other people. If you have a friend or acquaintance in the group, use them to slip your foot in the door.

7. Prepare conversation topics in advance – Before attempting to join a group conversation, do some prior reading to be up to date with current topics and subjects of discussion. Share opinions (keep the topics noncontroversial) and stick to popular topics such as entertainment, health, and sports. Be aware of the latest news that can pop up in the conversation. If something remarkable or important has happened in the day, there's a high chance it's going to be a topic of conversation at any social gathering. Add a brand new perspective or share some unique insights with the group. Personal preferences, experiences, travel, and interests make for interesting group conversation topics.

One of the most important aspects of a group conversation that several people overlook is not being nervous or fearful of silence. In our impatience to establish a quick rapport with everyone, we quit even before other people can process what we spoke. Give people an opportunity to know you, and don't be afraid of some silence. Allow them to understand align with you, and take their time to respond.

Again, when you are asking questions or picking random conversation topics, keep in mind that a group conversation is similar to layers of an onion. Every individual has multiple layers comprising different aspects of their life. Begin peeling off their first layer by sticking to a relatively safe question that they are comfortable answering publicly. This is the initial layer that they are happy to share with others. Then, come up with a follow-up conversation with the initial question. By doing this, you increase the prospect of them going a layer deeper when it comes to sharing about themselves.

When someone shares their problems or challenges by going into deeper layers, avoid trying to fix their problems. Do not give out simplistic solutions, quick-fixes, and advice. If you disagree with someone about an issue, put across your point in a healthy, respectful and empathetic manner. Appear genuinely curious and intrigued by a difference in opinion instead of pouncing on people that yours is the only way to look at it.

Learn to move away from past mistakes. Plenty of people suffer from social anxiety or lack of confidence in social situations owing to a blunder or blunders they made in the past. Evaluate your chances of repeating it. Are there high chances you'll repeat the same mistakes again now that you know better?

You won't make a mockery of yourself each time you approach a group or individual for communication. Learn from past mistakes rather than ruminating over them. Get out of this trap of guilt, regret, shame, and negativity. There's a bright future ahead where your social life is concerned. Go out there and make it happen.

I'll share something wonderful I picked up from a socially awkward friend to move past her regrets and guilt and develop more social confidence. After attending each social gathering or event, she makes a list of the ten best things that happened during the event or gathering. It includes ten new things she's grateful for after each event. Count as many amazing things as you can after attending a social event. It can be a new friend you made at the party or someone you were attracted to and want to date or a potential client you rubbed shoulders with at a gathering or something new you learned by interacting with a person. Gratitude changes your thought frequency from negative to positive in a matter of minutes. It will help you overcome negative feelings of the past and get into a more positive, confident and constructive frame of mind. This, in turn, will help you approach people with greater confidence, self-assuredness, and positivity.

8. Approaching people at conferences – One of the best tips I've picked up for approaching people at conferences and seminars is going up to a person (involved in a group discussion) who asked a good question. Talk to them about the question. It can be a nice icebreaker and a starting point. You can say something like, "I really liked that question you asked the speaker. And I think..." Build a conversation around it with the group. Chances are the person will be more than willing to accommodate you in the group, and even introduce himself/herself and his/her co-workers/associates. Ensure you add value to the conversation or add your own insights. You should be able to add your own interesting and unique two cents to the conversation.

Don't be shy of offering compliments and encouragement to group members. Everyone loves to have a positive person in their midst. If someone is particularly well-dressed, compliment them for their attire. If someone across as humorous and intelligent, compliment them for their sense of humor. Let people know what you appreciate about them to break the ice, and make them more receptive to what you speak.

This can be another good starting point for a conversation. Avoid over-doing though. A constant flow of compliments may sound insincere. The group may get a feeling that you are simply resorting to flattery to make headway or earn a breakthrough. The key is to keep it limited, sincere and specific. The more specific and detailed your compliments, the more sincere they sound. Instead of simply complimenting them for how wonderful their attire is, you can say something like, "the color compliments your skin tone perfectly" or "I love the color and the cuts on your outfit." Make it specific, so it comes across as a well-observed and thoughtful compliment rather than plain flattery.

9. *Request someone to accompany you* – A person I knew very closely followed this strategy during the initial days of his social anxiety recovery program (this was an extreme case though). Though he was suffering from acute social anxiety, people with milder social anxiety or plain low social confidence can also benefit from it. The person used to take along a trusted friend or family member to social gatherings during the early stages of his social interaction recovery plan.

If you fear to approach large groups, visiting unknown places or attending big events alone, request someone to accompany you in the beginning. Don't stick to them like Siamese twins and ignore everyone else though. They are just around for support and encouragement, not for you to latch on throughout the event. The idea or thought that someone is around to help you navigate the social situation can give you greater comfort and confidence in talking to strangers. Gradually, you'll learn to be on your own without assistance from others.

Even if you move gradually and slowly, take confident, self-assured steps in the right direction to make progress. You won't transform into a confident social being who is fully equipped to approach groups immediately. However, willpower, consistent effort, and relentless practice will get you there is no time.

CHAPTER 8

The Importance of Empathy

Empathy seems to be a unicorn in the communication world, yet it plays a huge part in effective communication. Empathy is simply being able to understand and share emotions with other people. It is made up of several different components, each of which works in its own place in the brain. You could look at empathy in three ways.

The first one is affective empathy. This means that you have the ability to your emotions with other people. People who have a lot of affective empathy are people who show strong visceral reactions to scary movies or violence on the news. They can feel the pain and fear of others within themselves when they see people in pain or fear.

The second is cognitive empathy. This type of empathy is having the ability to understand other people's emotions. A good example would be a psychologist who understands their client's emotions in a rational way but doesn't necessarily feel their client's emotions in a visceral sense.

Lastly, there is emotional regulation. This refers to how well a person is able to regulate their own emotions. For example, surgeons must be able to control their emotions while operating on them in order to do their job effectively.

Let's take another look at understanding empathy to help distinguish it from other similar ideas. For example, empathy means the person has to be self-aware, and they need to maintain a distinction between self and other. This is why empathy is different than imitation or mimicry.

There are quite a lot of animals that may show signs of mimicry or emotional contagion when they see other animals in pain. But without some form of self-awareness, and being able to differentiate self and other, it isn't necessarily empathy. Empathy isn't the same thing as sympathy, either. Sympathy is feeling concerned for a person who is suffering and having a desire to help them.

That being said, humans aren't the only species to feel empathy. In lab settings, it has been spotted in non-human primates and rats.

There are a lot of people who like to say that psychopaths lack empathy, but this isn't always true. In fact, psychopathy is actually more effective when the person has good cognitive empathic abilities. Basically, the psychopath needs to understand exactly what the victim is feeling when they are killing or torturing them. The skill that psychopaths lack is sympathy. They are completely fine with watching the person suffer and don't feel the need to help.

Research has also found that people who have psychopathic traits are great at regulating their own emotions.

Why Is Empathy Important?

The reason empathy is important is that it gives us the chance to understand how other people are feeling so that we are able to respond in an appropriate manner. It is most often connected with social behavior and there is plenty of research that shows that more empathy can lead to helpful behavior.

This isn't always the case, though. Empathy can also prevent social interactions, or cause a person to act in an immoral way. For example, a person who has witnessed a terrible car accident and becomes overwhelmed at the sight of the victims in severe pain is something less likely to help them.

Similarly, having strong empathetic feelings from family members or people in your own racial or social groups can lead to aggression or hate towards others who are seen as a threat. This is the reason why mothers will sometimes become "mama bears" when their child is in danger, whether real or not.

People who can easily read the emotions of others, like psychics, fortune-tellers, or manipulators, may use their skills to benefit their self through deceiving others.

What's interesting, those who have higher psychopathic traits will show more utilitarian responses in moral dilemmas, like with the footbridge problem. In this experiment, people were faced with the decision of whether to push another off of the bridge to stop a train that was getting ready to kill five people who were on the track.

The psychopath would push the person off the bridge. This goes along with the utilitarian philosophy that says saving the lives of five people by killing one is good. It could be argued that people with psychopathic tendencies have higher morals than normal people, who would likely not push that person off of the bridge, because they aren't as influenced by their emotions when they make their decisions.

Measurement of Empathy

Empathy is typically measured through a self-reported questionnaire like the Questionnaire for Cognitive and Affective Empathy or Interpersonal Reactivity Index. These normally ask people to say whether or not they agree with certain statements in order to measure empathy.

With the QCAE, it asks things like "It affects me very much when one of my friends is upset," which helps to give a score for affective empathy. The QCAE figures out cognitive empathy by placing a value on statements like, "I try to look at everybody's side of a disagreement before I make a decision."

Through this particular questionnaire, researchers have discovered that those who scored higher with affective empathy has more grey matter, which is a group of nerve cells, in the part of the brain known as the anterior insula.

This is the area of the brain that is involved in regulating negative and positive emotions by using environmental stimulants with automatic and visceral bodily sensations. People who had higher scores in cognitive empathy had greater grey matter in the dorsomedial prefrontal cortex.

This is the area of the brain that is normally activated during cognitive processes, like the Theory of Mind, which is having the ability to connect mental beliefs to others and yourself. It also means that you understand that others have perspectives, intentions, desires, and beliefs that are different than your own.

Selective Empathy?

Research has found that people normally feel more empathy for people within their own group, like those in a single ethnic group. There was one study performed that scanned the brains of Caucasian and Chinese participants as they watched a video of people of the same ethnic group in pain. They also watched a video of people of a different ethnic group in pain.

They discovered that the anterior cingulate cortex, which is activated when people witness somebody in pain, wasn't as active when they were watching the videos of a different ethnic group in pain. There have been other studies that had discovered that the brain areas involved with empathy tend to be less active when they watched people pain who acted unfairly. They have also noticed activation in brain areas that are involved in subjective pleasure, like the ventral striatum, when people watch a rival sports team lose.

Yet, people don't always feel less empathy for people who are not a part of their group. In more recent studies, students were asked to give money or electrical shocks to other students who attended the same or a different school. They were also undergoing a brain scan during this as well.

The areas of the brain involved in rewarding people were more active when they gave a reward to those from their school, but the parts of the brain involved in hurting others were equally as active.

This corresponds with observations people have made in daily life. We typically feel happier if a person in our group wins something, but we are unlikely to hurt a person just because they aren't a part of our group, race, or culture. In general, in-group bias tends to be more about love instead of out-group hate.

There are some situations, though, where it would be helpful to feel less empathy for a certain group. For example, during war, it could be helpful to feel less empathy for those you are supposed to kill, especially if they are interested in harming you.

There was a brain imaging study performed to investigate this. People were asked to watch videos of a violent game where a person was shooting an innocent person or an enemy soldier. As they watch the videos, people would have to pretend that they were actually killing real people. The lateral orbitofrontal cortex, which is normally active when a person harms somebody, was active when an innocent person was shot. The more guilt that the person felt about shooting somebody, the more this area responded.

However, this area of the brain wasn't activated when a person shot the enemy soldier. The results helped scientists to figure out how people regulated their emotions. It also showed them how the brain worked when harming people was seen as justified.

This may well help provide more insights into how people can end up becoming desensitized to violence or why there are some people who feel less or more guilty about hurting others.

The empathetic brain has evolved to become very adaptive in certain situations. Having empathy is helpful because it helps us to understand other people, but there are times when switching of empathy might be beneficial when it comes to protecting your life, or another's life.

Empathy in Communication

We've covered a lot of scientific information about empathy and how it affects our daily lives, but we need to look at exactly how it helps with communication. The biggest benefit of bringing empathy into a conversation is being able to handle a confrontation. This is a situation that nobody likes to find their self in, but it happens from time to time. People get angry, and then the conversation turns into a shouting match, but with empathy, it doesn't have to.

Anger is a normal emotion and is meant to be used as a way to communicate something. Anger can also push people away, but you really want is to be heard and connect with people. The same is true for a person who chooses a passive-aggressive behavior instead of a direct one. It's aggression, whether straightforward or not. This is where empathy plays an important role. Whether or not it is anger rearing its ugly head in conversation, you can use these six steps to take the conversation back to neutral ground.

1. **Focus on what is actually happening and allow yourself to become more self-aware.**

If you are the one that is angry or upset, give yourself some time. Trying to communicate while in a frustrated state won't turn out well. Words don't come out right and things that shouldn't be said, get said. Extremely emotions hijack the brain. When the emotions centers of the brain become overactive, people have a lot harder time thinking logically. Allow yourself to calm down or cool off, and then see if you are able to think more clearly and communicate yourself more effectively.

If it is the other person becoming emotional, the first thing you should NOT do is tell them to calm down. Never, in the history of the world, has this ever helped a person calm down. If the person begins to cry, sit quietly and let them cry, give them a moment. If they are becoming angry, give them a moment to express their anger if need be, and fight the urge to become defensive. Let them know that you would like to understand how they are feeling. Let them know that it is okay that they feel this way. Ask a lot of questions, and if need be, let them know that you can talk later once they feel ready.

2. Understand your emotions.

Whether you are the emotional one or not, you need to figure out why you are feeling what you are feeling. There are times where we think we feel frustrated, but in actuality, we are experiencing sorrow, pain, or rejection. Once you have figure out what you are feeling, then you can communicate it better and help the other person.

3. Figure out if there is some form of misplaced blame.

It is extremely easy to blame a person or situation for how we are feeling. People can feel overworked, hungry, unhappy in their marriage, stressed, or tired, and then they assign all of the blame onto the first situation or person that they encounter. It is likely somebody close to them as well. This is why, if a person gets angry at you, don't become defensive because it's not likely that you are the actual thing they are mad at.

4. Become more curious.

When you focus on your anger, frustration, or sadness keeps all of your focus on yourself. Research has found that negative emotions cause a person to become self-centered. This means that you have no room for another person's perspective because you are locked into your own view. People don't take the time to consider what the other person may be going through. This is when curiosity should be brought in. Become curious about the reason why a person is acting a certain way. Instead of being confrontational, show genuine interest into why the person feels or acts a certain way. The majority of people don't go around with evil intentions, but a lot of people do make mistakes and upset other people. Chances are, the person didn't act purposefully.

5. Have compassion.

When you take the time to ask "why," you are allowing communication to take place, and you are showing respect and consideration for the way they act, feel, and think. This will help to create a better relationship and understanding based upon empathy and compassion.

6. Communicate with skill.

When communicating with a person who is upset, or if you are upset, use "I" statements. This removes confrontation. But you want to also make sure that you give the other person a chance to share their perspective. This should be done through simple questions, again, to make sure they don't feel like you are attacking them. You want to be curious and not accusatory.

CHAPTER 9

Improve your Communication Using Emotional Management

Emotional management or EQ exists as the aptitude towards sensing and handling feelings. An advanced EQ helps people to interact well, reduce their stress and worry, defuse conflicts, perk up dealings, have concern for other people, and the gift of knocking out the trials that come with life. It is vital in interaction because feelings hold a big part in communication.

The skill of being aware of feelings or emotional awareness can help people succeed when relating to others. It helps in noting the feelings of others and how these feelings influence the manner they speak or communicate. EQ and emotional maturity are key aspects in keeping wholesome affairs, be it in marriage, friendship, or at the workplace.

Instead of blaming someone else for a problem or action, these emotionally mature people seek to revise the action or solve the problem. They hold themselves liable for their choices and actions without the need to lie in tough settings. Instead, they confront the truth head-on.

In any quarrel, they refrain from making any attack on the person and simply address the matter at hand. They are cautious in speaking and ensure their calmness by thinking before speaking. They respect limits and never depend on the childish defense process of rebound. If you are emotionally intelligent, then you can simply detect and control your own feelings.

You can sense emotions, besides proactively acting in response, instead of reactively. And because people with high EQ are in control of their feelings, they can put them well into words. They accept these feelings as they are and do not even try to disguise them by way of some other emotion. They use them as needed in terms of thinking or solving problems, mostly in dealings.

After all, when you have a dispute with someone, it is normal to feel a certain emotive response, which is adverse by and large. Hey, nothing is wrong with going through an adverse emotional response, but the way you use this response later makes all the honor or disgrace. Indeed, it requires some change in your mindset and can be quite hard to perfect.

Still, starting to tackle these settings in a mature, as well as wise manner, is where the wisdom sets off, and all else is a change for the better from there. Emotional management and maturity work together. You need your emotional management skills to recognize your feelings. Simultaneously, your emotional maturity will help you not to show your feelings reactively.

And this is essential in managing relationships. To properly find these qualities in a partner, you have to ensure that you possess those skills to start with. Why? Well, without those skills in you, you will not be capable of recognizing and acknowledging in others whatever you need yourself. So, work first on yourself, as this is the initial step in creating healthy and long-lasting relationships.

When you have accomplished this, help your spouse or partner work on his or her emotional maturity and intelligence. Remember that emotional maturity and intelligence requires constant, conscious training. Also, there may be instances when you will not perfect this skill. With diligence and dedication, though, you will eventually develop it and find it as a true indication of your growth. And when you can do this with your spouse or partner, that is what I meant when I said, "grow up together.

How to Work on Bettering Your Emotional Management

Some people possess an incredibly great IQ but minimal EQ, like a nutty scientist who cannot match his clothes. Other people possess incredibly high emotional intelligence but low general intelligence. And this can be seen in a street vendor, who cannot even write his name, yet can somehow convince you to buy his merchandise even when you may not personally need it.

Perhaps, this is among the reasons why psychologists sometimes assert that EQ is actually far important than IQ. The problem is that, unlike IQ, it is not stable and it's difficult to measure EQ. On top of that, it is mostly subjective. In contrast, EQ can be made better as compared to the stable IQ. So, you can develop it as you would work on your muscles or expertise and watch it grow.

Most of all, you do not need a high IQ to do this! Cool, right? The question now is how. Technically speaking, the skills drawn in EQ are awareness and regulation of one's self, motivation, empathy, besides social skills. And all these require patience, appreciation, gratitude, respect, and anger management. It would be best to first work on the last five qualities to facilitate the acquisition of the five first mentioned skills. So, let me present them to you in such an order.

Patience

This virtue assists in building empathy towards other people. If things do not go as you want them to, instead of entertaining that feeling of frustration, learn patience. Try seeing things and settings as a blessing in disguise or develop a positive mindset to have a happier life. When in an exasperating conversation, try listening well to the speaker and give yourself time to process your thoughts before saying anything.

A person needs enough patience to maintain harmony in his private, professional, and social life. And in relationships, patience is an essential element. By grasping the impact of patience, anyone can create peace in his relationships, which can transform his life for the better. You can be more patient in your relationship by first knowing your partner as an imperfect person like you are.

Next, accept the shortcomings of your partner or spouse. At the same time, let your spouse know you, as well, through regular communication. Make sure to listen to your partner when he is communicating verbally or nonverbally. Allow your spouse to be free to show you his real self and dedicate some time together, even in silence.

If your partner has the tendency to be grumpy, do not react in the same manner. For as long as you keep your communication lines open at all times, and you are determined to develop more patience, you will get by.

Appreciation, Gratitude, and Respect

Have you observed how the lack of appreciation looks like an increasing problem with all pairs, married or not, but have been living together for some years? If you believe that your partner has stopped appreciating your presence in this life, then you would agree with me when I say that appreciation is important in all healthy relationships!

As a human being, I believe that we constantly thirst for attention, which can only be done through appreciation. The problem begins when we fail to notice that we are slipping into the custom of taking our other half for granted. When this happens, we stop showing care and appreciation for our spouse. This causes other problems, like arguments, feelings of frustration, and resentment.

Then suddenly, probably after a big fight, we begin wondering if the relationship can be worked out or heading out of the door. Let us recall a common and simple scenario. Your spouse always brings your children to school and fetches them for home each and every school day. It has become a routine that you never showed any appreciation for.

Honestly, tell me. Are you not grateful that your partner is there to do this every school day since your children started going to school? Can you imagine its effect on your daily life if he simply stopped doing it for one day? Of course, you will need to make changes in your schedule for the day to accommodate this task. Probably, you will have to out of bed earlier than usual.

Would you be happy not watching your morning news show on TV because you also need to drop off the kids before going to work? Then, pick them up again from work in time after school? Yes, it is something simple, but can suddenly become important once not done! I remember asking a work colleague whose wife does this task if he ever thanked her for diligently doing it.

Guess his response! He frowned at me and replied, "What is there to thank her for that when they are understood to be done anyway?" I smiled and slowly walked away, knowing that my work colleague thinks that he is doing bigger things than what his spouse does. And that is where the stability in relationships begins to go off the scale. Appreciation remains vital to any relationship.

Valuing someone can make them feel happy about whatever they are doing. And that can make a difference in their existence. They feel better about themselves, urging them to keep on with fresh vigor, and strengthening their relationship. Interested in knowing if your spouse lacks appreciation? It is actually easy as certain signs imply being undervalued in a relationship, as follows:

1. There are now arguments over trivial things;
2. Lately, your spouse starts getting more emotional;
3. Perhaps, they talk less now as compared to before;
4. Opinions are no longer asked;
5. Plans are made without consulting the other;
6. Less enthusiastic about occasions, such as anniversaries and birthday;
7. Poor sex life; and,
8. Preference for more time away from each other.

Appreciation has two aspects, specifically one based on focus and the other on time. Time-based appreciation exists slightly like a puzzle as you either turn out to be angrier with the behavior of your partner or become more patient. Now, which turns out is an issue of outlook. Acceptance begins from your awareness that things remain not likely towards changing over time, hence, you turn out more accepting.

When this happens, it is easier for you to appreciate what he/she does. If you alter your viewpoint, you may get even used to their most irritating ways and find some importance in them. Besides, this lets you focus on whatever makes them happy. So, in what way can you display your appreciation towards your partner? At hand are certain things you can try, as follows:

1. Admit what you are fond of about your spouse, his family, and friends;

2. Appreciate all that adds importance to your bond and regularly tell your spouse about it;

3. Compliment him on simple matters, such as saying "I love the way that printed tie enhances your professional look!"

4. Enjoy your moments together by being lively while appreciating one another;

5. Focus fully on whatever your partner is saying and make eye contact to assure him that you value whatever he is telling you;

6. Thank him for little stuff, such as ironing your clothes, doing the laundry, or cooking food when you feel too tired or lazy to do them. Examples are the following lines:

a. "I am really grateful for your washing up the dishes after supper."

b. "Honey, I love the way you help me prepare my things each morning while I dress up for the office. It makes me feel so special!"

c. "Thank you so much for coming into my life, dear. I wonder how I can go through life without you by my side!"

7. Most importantly, regularly express your gratitude and affection for your spouse.

Healthy relationships stand those that keep growing and, in terms of love, appreciating your partner is never sufficient. When you invest so much in relations, it feels delightful to receive an acknowledgment for the effort. So, make appreciating your spouse a priority towards keeping the spark perky.

Anger Management

When you create a romantic bond, you carry this out with your unique personalities formed by your previous relationships. So, each has developed notions about the way the beloved should react to your desires, needs, and expectations. Additionally, you have well-established patterns that include the manner you manage annoyance when your loved one appears to ignore your desires, needs, and expectations.

It is then unsurprising that, irrespective of how loving your relationship is, at times anger and conflict happens. And this is particularly challenging when both or one of you are prone to irritation. While having conflicts now and then is usual for couples, once they become intense and frequent, they can negatively impact the physical, mental, and family well-being of a household.

The prospective for such effect especially arises once both or one of the partners is susceptible to anger. And destructive anger within relationships can cause sadness, increased dissatisfaction, and thoughts of abuse, isolation, and eventually divorce. Irrespective of the way you studied on dealing with disagreements, it is essential to bear in mind that there are specific flairs that support positive management of conflict, including recovering from conflicts.

Always bring to mind that the nastiest time to quarrel is when you are furiously angry because it is when you are more prone to concentrate on your personal grievances and not ready to listen to your partner. So, allow me to share with you a clear set of tactics to deal with conflict that is rooted in self-awareness, mindfulness, and empathy for your partner and yourself. I urge you to share these strategies with your spouse and have a signed pledge to observe them as we did.

1. Commit to practicing healthy anger as the foundation for constructively dealing with conflicts in your relationship. So, when your partner remains quick to anger, it is best not to respond in anger as well, and instead listen to him. If you are the one who is quick to anger, take time outs.

2. Only when both of you have controlled your anger can you carry out a proper sharing in a concession and solve your problem. This means that each should focus on specific actions, not on statements uttered by an angry partner. Moreover, when both are sufficiently relaxed, then it is time for you to discuss your differences.

3. Both should agree to stop the discussion and have a time-out when any partner feels too worked up or intensely uncomfortable. Additionally, set limits regarding using bad language, yelling, behaving in an abusive manner, or threatening. In our case, we agreed to use the word "Time-out" to signal the need to cease further argument for a while.

4. Ideally, it is best to resume whatever activity is ongoing or planned before the conflict. In certain cases, though, solitude is

needed. When this happens, the person wanting some time alone just utters our agreed phrase of "Tea Break."

Generally, we just comfortably proceed with our activity together without talking about the disagreement until we are both calm. When the magic words "Tea Break" are spoken though, the speaker will have our bedroom all for himself until he comes out or calls out for the other to come in. We have agreed on this instead of leaving home to prevent triggering the other to feel further anxiety, especially when sensitive to the issue abandoned.

5. When we decide towards stopping a discussion with no resolution, we generally resume the talk when both are sufficiently relaxed. This is because we have made a commitment to solving issues. And if the feeling of anger escalates on the next discussion, we stop to calm down, as well as trying again a few days later.

6. If our argument concerns important issues, unsettled conflicts will pop up again. So, failing to talk about identified issues only damages this entire arrangement. Nevertheless, we also have to be aware of time limitations since both of us are working.

7. Thus, our agreed discussion period is a maximum of an hour. If unresolved, then it is resumed later in the same day, the day after, or any other agreed day when both have no other commitments and are calm. We also set rules on conducting discussions, such as never in front of the children or in our bedroom.

8. And when issues are fully addressed, we individually apologize for our respective share to the conflict and tension. In this way, we reaffirm our respect, trust, and love for each other.

These guidelines have made my marriage stand the test of time. I am sharing this with you with the prayer that it will help you somehow bridge any communication gap you may have with your partner. Having differences is expected once you go into a deep relationship. And once they take place, your challenge is to communicate constructively.

Managing conflict through this manner remains a crucial ingredient aimed at a more pleasing relationship. So, take time to appease yourself enough towards thinking about whatever you are annoyed about. Remember that your annoyance is revealing something about your personality. Although the anger is frequently aimed at your spouse, it is always more concerning you than concerning your spouse.

Awareness

Without this trait, trying to handle your emotions is like sitting inside a tiny dinghy without direction atop the ocean of your personal emotions totally at the fancy of the tides of whatever exists happening each moment. Having no idea of where you are going, all you could do is yell for assistance.

Awareness of one's self involves understanding your actions on three stages, specifically, what you are doing; the way you feel regarding it; and the hardest of them all, figuring out whatever you do not see about yourself. In the first stage, we tend to do things nowadays on autopilot.

For example, wake up each day to wash your face, brush your teeth, prepare breakfast, wake up the kids and hubby, feed the pets, take the kids to school, go to the gym, market, or home, and so on. To develop self-awareness, you can try scheduling time or a day to break the monotony. For example, setting 10 minutes in the day to just think of your life and how you are feeling.

Once you really focus on your feelings, which is the second stage, it can be scary in the beginning. You might realize how often you are actually pretty depressed or go through a great deal of anxiety. At this moment, it is important not to judge the feelings that arise as it can just make things worse.

Instead, have faith that whatever emotion stays there holds a good purpose for being there even when you cannot remember that reason. Once you spot all the uncomfortable stuff you are feeling, you will begin to sense where your personal vulnerable points are.

For instance, when I am speaking and someone interrupts me, I really get irritated. Upon being aware of these points, I can start figuring out how do deal with my emotions and do something about them, which is the final stage.

CONCLUSION

Your next move needs to be putting some of these steps into action. Set aside all of your worries and anxiety and get down to the business of saving your relationship. Forget all the drama and negative talk you hear and break everything down into common-sense steps. Marriages and relationships that were considered a lost cause are now thriving after making only a few changes. You will see results right away without spending huge amounts of money on counselors and marriage therapists.

Find a comfortable starting point and begin making changes that will be life-altering. Prepare yourself to be amazed at how easy and enjoyable some of the steps can be. Each day will result in building more trust and understanding from your partner. If both of you are committed to making the changes, the sky is the limit.

Learning to navigate the world as a couple never came with a handbook – until now. You will have the edge in knowing what it takes to make it through any crisis and problem that a couple can face. You'll be able to come out winners every time!

Finally, if you found this book useful in any way, a review on Amazon is always appreciated!

Documenting your journey as a couple can be a fun activity that gives you and your family a wealth of information to look back on over the years. You can capture all of those important moments that become fuzzy memories over time. Almost every home, decades ago contained bunches of photo albums. A couple's journal goes beyond by allowing you to document how people feelings about experiences. You can some playful elements that give each partners perspective on the other. It will be a cherished item for any children you have to see their parent's relationship unfold with each page.

Document Milestones

Special occasions like birthdays and anniversaries are to be expected and should be documented. What about times you've graduated from college or training programs? You can add things like the birth of children, moving to a new home, buying a new car, adding a pet to the family, or purchasing a boat. All of the items and occasions mentioned will begin to build a picture of your life. Add pictures, programs, or any other documents that give more information about each milestone. Adding specific details like locations and who is involved will help you recall the occasions and events easily.

Document Vacations

Do you and your partner love to travel for vacations? Make sure and add some space to document these great adventures. It's another area of the journal that will benefit from any images you have, restaurant menus, travel brochures, plane ticket stubs, and more. Where did you go and explain how you made the choice? What did you do while at the vacation destination? List any funny, happy, sad, or aggravating experiences. Document your vacation travel, even if it was only a few miles from home. You can just as much fun and adventure as touring the pyramids in Egypt.

Ask and Answer Daily Questions

Get your partner involved daily in documenting your lives together. Think of and write down a question each day that is both thought-provoking and makes a point. Keep them on the lighter side and pick subjects that will help reveal their personalities. It can be difficult to maintain a daily Q&A but give it a try. You and your partner will begin to look forward to the unexpected question that awaits their attention. Give full answers. Don't get skimpy on the answers just because you had a long or hard day at work. The better you explain things, the clearer it is for those that don't have the benefit of being able to take family vacations.

Likes and Compliments

Add all of the likes of you and partner in the couple's journal to memorialize all of their favorite things. Be sure and speak up on the page with some of your own. You can also create a space within the journal to compliment your partner. Put your thinking cap on and list every little thing you can think of that you like and love about your partner. You can add to this as you go. Have your partner do the same thing about you, featuring every good thing they can think of that endears you in their world.

Daily Recording of Important Events

Every good couple's journal will have areas that are completely dedicated to bringing both specialty subjects or events and the daily grind. Be sure and add little details like the funniest thing to happen that day, any struggles that were overcome, fun activities, and any other major details that make the journal interesting. You will have a lifetime of memories compiled that is incomparable to anything else. Save ticket stubs for movies, concerts and other events you attend and paste them in the journal. You don't have to save everything, but a few to make looking back enjoyable.

Bucket List for Two

Where are all the places you'd love to travel and things you'd love to do as a couple before you die? Create a space in the journal that details all of the wants and desires you both have to see and experience the world. It can be grand plans that never come to fruition, but it gives you real direction in understanding the dreams of your partner. Your partner might dream of climbing Mount Everest together, but you can probably settle for taking a nice hike up a smaller mountain trail on your next vacation.

Sharing Special Goals and Plans

Journaling any special goals and plans you and your partner make is a little different than the bucket list. It should be filled with your goals of home, family, career, vacations, and where you see your life in 5, 10, or 25-years. It can be a comforting area to read if you are experiencing conflict and relationship problems. It can redirect your energies towards working things out. When you can see in black and white how far you've already come, it gives you added energy to go that much farther.

Challenge Your Partner

Being able to present your partner with a challenge can be a fun addition to your couple's journal. Wives can challenge husbands to baking cakes or making a specific type of candy. Husbands can challenge wives to change the oil in the car. It doesn't have to be anything specific. Husbands might already be great at baking cakes and wives at changing vehicle oil. Pick something that each is not accustomed to doing and watch the hilarity begin. It's another spot that would be improved with added images. Get creative but be safe with the activities chosen. You can do these many times over the years.

Ingram Content Group UK Ltd.
Milton Keynes UK
UKHW022212240723
425713UK00006B/210